FASHION JEWELRY

crimped
w/ softflex
: french
wire

Toggle
clasp

- Natural
stones

FASHION JEWELRY

A Beginner's Guide to Jewelry Making

Courtney Legenhausen

of Lotus Jewelry Studio

LARK

New York

An Imprint of Sterling Publishing Co., Inc.
1166 Avenue of the Americas
New York, NY 10036

ISBN 978-1-4547-1032-5

Distributed in Canada by Sterling Publishing Co., Inc.
c/o Canadian Manda Group, 664 Annette Street
Toronto, Ontario, Canada M6S 2C8
Distributed in the United Kingdom by GMC Distribution Services
Castle Place, 166 High Street, Lewes, East Sussex, England BN7 1XU
Distributed in Australia by NewSouth Books
45 Beach Street, Coogee, NSW 2034, Australia

For information about custom editions, special sales, and premium and corporate purchases,
please contact Sterling Special Sales at 800-805-5489 or specialsales@sterlingpublishing.com.

Manufactured in China

2 4 6 8 10 9 7 5 3 1

www.sterlingpublishing.com
larkcrafts.com

Photography by Liz Mathews
Design by Patrice Sheridan

Dedicated to my loving husband, Erik Legenhausen.
You are the best jeweler I know and
have always been unwavering in your support.
I love you.

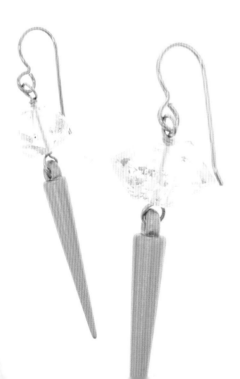

Whether you are new to jewelry making or an experienced crafter, this book will teach you the fundamentals of jewelry construction. Through detailed instructions and step-by-step photos, we will explore the many ways to craft beautiful jewelry using minimal tools and basic techniques. Get inspired by the quality pieces you can create in the comfort of your home, using simple tools and materials found at your local craft store.

Jewelry making is a fun and creative way to make personalized, wearable art that will be appreciated for years to come. The craft dates back to the beginning of recorded history and produces some of the most widely used articles in fashion and self-expression to date. This book provides direction on how to get started and gives detailed explanations of the required tools and materials through a collection of step-by-step projects for earrings, bracelets, and necklaces.

Together we will explore bead stringing, simple wire wrapping and pearl knotting techniques, and applying finishes to metals. In addition to the projects, you will learn about the various tools and materials as well as helpful and important tips and information to become skilled in the art of jewelry making. For a very small investment, you can make impressive jewelry that can be shared and passed down for years to come!

Sometimes the most difficult aspect of any new project is knowing where to start. Every designer I have had the pleasure of meeting has his or her own method of bringing about creations. All I can offer is what works for me and how I turn my ideas into tangible items.

Everything starts with a sketch. I often carry a small sketchbook so that I can record my ideas the moment I feel inspired. When I fail to record my ideas in the moment, the thought or picture gets lost. For a while, I tried to convince myself that I would remember these grand ideas without recording them, and each time I was proven wrong. After learning that lesson, I created the habit of drawing my designs at the precise moment I feel inspired.

I love to have these moments of divine intervention, when ideas flood into my brain like a river when a dam breaks. But let's be real: most times, trying to come up with a new and innovative design is like squeezing blood from a stone. During times when I feel my design sense is in a rut, I fall back on the techniques I learned in jewelry school. The biggest lesson here is that you can find inspiration for design anywhere.

Nature is a huge source of inspiration for me. The colors and textures of a beautiful landscape often provide me with endless ideas for new and exciting pieces. Second to Mother Nature is human nature—how people dress, how they walk, where they live, and such. Humans are fascinating to me. We are all so different—yet so alike. Next, I pull from my worldly travels: places I've seen with brightly colored buildings or ornate architecture, a beautifully woven basket, or the way a mother carries her child on her back. There are outlines, textures, and extraordinary color palettes everywhere.

The next step in my process is weeding through my ideas and deciding on ones that are most on point with today's styles and trends. As a business owner, I ultimately need to make jewelry that is relevant in the current marketplace. Prior to being a businesswoman, I would make things for the simple reason that they were aesthetically pleasing to me. When I'm designing a piece for the purpose of selling it, I have to consider many facets: What will be the profit margin? What type of person will purchase this? Can this be given as a gift? And so on.

The final stage in my process is constructing my piece and bringing my drawing to life. There are times my drawings do not match my vision once the piece is created. This is the point where I either tweak the design or scratch the whole thing and start over. Other times, my creations turn out exactly as I had hoped or, at times, more beautiful than I imagined. This step in the process is always the most satisfying. It has taken many years to develop the patience to work my process from a sketch, through refinement and consideration, and finally to creation. I find that when I fall back to my old habits of creating before making a plan and considering it thoroughly, the design either falls short or I end up wasting a lot of time and materials.

I encourage you to develop your own method of design. After all, it is the foundation of what you will do as a jewelry maker. We are not just crafters; we are artists. And any good artist needs to understand the concept of design and how to bring that forth.

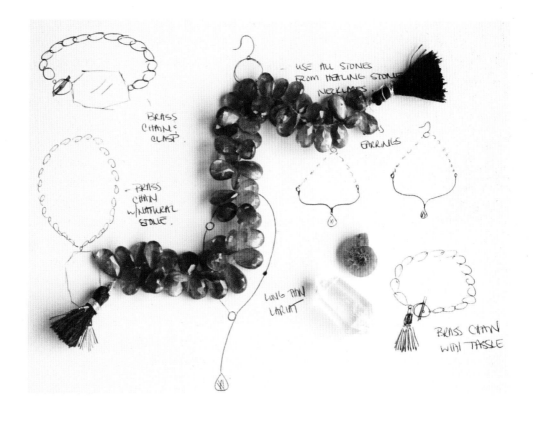

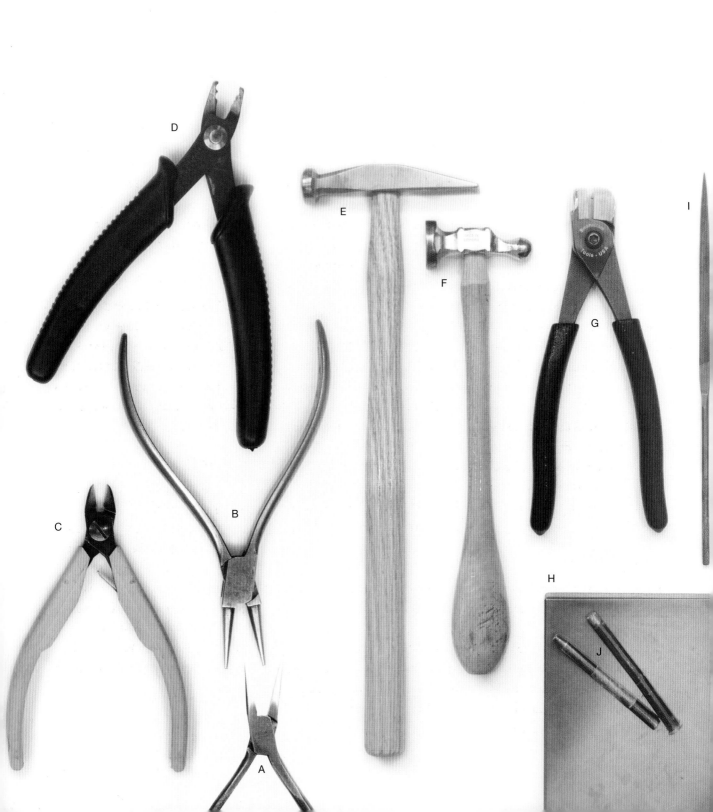

Tools

A. Flat-Nose Pliers

These pliers' jaws have flush surfaces, which make them very versatile when crafting jewelry. They are often used to hold things in place and to create bends in wire. It will be helpful to have two of these pliers available for certain projects.

B. Round-Nose Pliers

Round-nose pliers are an essential tool used in jewelry making. They have cylindrical tips that help create bends, curves, and loops in wire and other materials.

C. Wire Cutters

Flush wire cutters are preferred over non-flush cutters. Flush wire cutters have one flush side and one beveled side; the flush side will make blunt cuts in wire, string, and other materials.

D. Crimping Pliers

Crimping pliers are used for folding and closing metal crimp beads. The jaws have two notches, or "stations." The station farthest from the tip creates a crease down the center of the crimp bead. The second station, closest to the tip, assists in folding the creased crimp bead closed.

E. Goldsmith Hammer

This is an all-purpose hammer specially designed for jewelry work. One side of the hammer head is flat and the other side is chisel-shaped, making it an ideal tool for riveting, shaping, and forming. It is important to have a smooth finish on the flat head of your hammer when forging, to avoid making unnecessary marks in your metal.

F. Chasing Hammer

A chasing hammer has a large face for flattening and a ball-peen side for riveting and metal design. The ball-peen side provides a highly defined hammered finish when applied to metal. The flat side can be used in striking metal stamps; however, this action will mar the face of the hammer slightly.

G. Hole-Punching Pliers

This important tool assists in creating a smooth, clean hole in a variety of materials. These are great for novice jewelers who do not have access to a flex shaft or Dremel® tool for drilling holes through metal sheet and wire.

H. Steel Block

This flat, solid steel surface is used as a work foundation when applying hammered textures and stamped finishes to metal. It is important to have a smooth finish on your steel block prior to hammering metal on its surface, to avoid unnecessary marks in your metal.

I. Flat Needle-Nose File

Flat files are used in metal working and woodworking. They are made of hard steel and contain a series of cross-section teeth that cut and remove wood and metal. In jewelry making, files are used to shape and smooth metal.

J. Steel Stamps

There are hundreds of steel stamps available that can be used to create designs in metal. They are typically made of hard steel and have a design on one end and a blunt surface on the other. When you place the stamp end on the metal and strike the blunt end of the stamp with a hammer, the stamp imprints its design onto the metal surface.

Metals & Components

A. Sheet & Wire

Sheet and wire are available in a variety of metals. The most commonly used metals for jewelry are silver, gold, gold-filled, copper, brass, and nickel. They are all available in a range of gauges that designate thickness and diameter (see page 169 for sheet and wire gauge charts). Gold and sterling silver are the most widely used metals, but other materials, such as platinum, tungsten, and stainless steel, can be used to construct jewelry. Copper can often turn the skin green, and nickel produces an allergic reaction in some who wear it.

See page 47 for additional information on working with metal materials.

B. Spring Ring Clasp

This is a circular clasp with a small spring, which is compressed when a tiny lever is pulled back, revealing a gap in the ring. This clasp is used widely in this book.

C. Toggle Clasp

This clasp consists of two parts: a solid ring and a T-shaped bar. The clasp is fastened by placing the T-shaped bar through the ring and resting the bar across the ring to hold it closed. Toggle clasps are very commonly used in bracelets because they are easy for a person to open and close without assistance.

D. Jump Rings

These small rings come in varying diameters and thicknesses. A jump ring may have a cut so it can be opened and closed, allowing it to be used in attaching jewelry components together. Closed jump rings are referred to as soldered rings.

E. Chain

A chain is a connected flexible series of metal links. Chains are widely used in jewelry construction either as a means to hang a necklace pendant or as embellishments to jewelry. Chains come in many different styles, including cable chains, curb chains, ball chains, snake chains, and omega chains.

F. Ear Wires

These are earring findings that most commonly come in a question mark shape and have a small loop at the bottom. Ear wires are used in the construction of dangle earrings.

G. Head Pins

A head pin is a metal post, or "pin," with a small, flat "head" on one end. The head is used as a stopper for beads placed on the pin, which allows you to create a loop in the remaining wire to be used in dangle earrings or other dangling components.

H. Flower Beads

Metal flower beads are often used to create patterns and embellishments in beaded jewelry. They are available in a range of metals, including silver, gold, and brass, and create a beautiful texture in beaded jewelry.

B

G

H

E

D

F

C

A

Gemstones

Pearl

Gemstones

Beads

Beads are available in a seemingly endless variety of shapes, colors, materials, and designs. Humans have been creating beads since as early as 70,000 BCE, and bead making has been an integral part in revealing the early history of humans and their behaviors. Beads have been used in the construction of jewelry throughout history. Below is a minimal list of the most commonly used beads and their materials. Bead sizes are often given in millimeters. You can view additional information on page 171, including bead sizes and shapes.

A. Glass *Not Shown

Glass beads are often an economical choice and are available in many colors, sizes, shapes, and opacities. Most of the bead shapes available in today's market are offered in glass. Some glass beads are coveted by collectors, such as Venetian and handblown glass.

B. Metal *Not Shown

Beads are available in a wide variety of metals, including sterling silver, gold, brass, nickel, pewter, vermeil, and copper, to name a few. They are most commonly created through a casting process, where molten metal is poured into a mold.

C. Pearl

Genuine pearls are formed within the shells of mollusks and are composed of a combination of minerals. When a foreign object enters the mollusk, it is coated with aragonite or calcite over a period of time, which creates the texture, luster, and color found in pearls today. Cultured pearls are made by a farming process, in which glass beads are inserted into mollusks, which greatly expedites the process of forming the pearls' outer layer.

D. Gemstones

Gemstone beads are my favorite material to work with when creating beaded jewelry. The colors, textures, weight, and luster of natural stone beads are unmatched. Stone beads are made of natural materials mined from the earth and are cut and formed into many sizes and shapes. They are often given facets to bring out the stone's natural shine and luster. Heat treatment, or coating, is a commonly used practice to bring out a more vibrant color. Stones provide quality and refinement to your beaded jewelry and are one of the more expensive options when purchasing materials. See page 170 for a stone chart.

Tip: The purist in me does not recommend using plastic beads for jewelry, which is why it is not mentioned in the above list of bead options. When you are investing the time to make jewelry, it is important that you strive to have the highest-quality product in the end; therefore, I never use plastic beads in my jewelry creations.

Stringing Supplies

A. Flexible Beading Wire

Flexible beading wire is constructed of either 21 or 49 microwoven stainless steel wires within a nylon coating. Flexible beading wire provides high durability to your beaded jewelry while allowing it to be soft and fluid. It comes in a variety of thicknesses, including 0.014-inch, 0.019-inch, and 0.024-inch diameters.

Tip: I prefer to use Soft Flex® over similar products because I have found that similar products easily bend, creating kinks that are hard to remove. Soft Flex holds its original shape much better and is not as easily damaged.

B. Silk Thread

There is a variety of silk available for jewelry making. I highly recommend Griffin silk products, especially for novice jewelry makers. Their silk is sold in a range of thicknesses (I use no. 4, or the 0.60 mm size, most often) and comes in a wide selection of colors. Griffin silk thread is sold in lengths of two meters and has a needle attached at one end. The needle is the same thickness as the thread, or thinner, which is extremely useful when stringing beads with very small holes.

Tip: It is very important to stretch silk thread prior to using it in the construction of your jewelry. If you fail to pre-stretch your silk, you will find that your jewelry pieces stretch over time and develop slack.

C. Nylon Thread

Nylon thread is similar to silk thread but has a stiffer, more rigid texture. It is also available in varying colors and thicknesses. I recommend Griffin nylon products, for similar reasons stated above about Griffin silk products.

Tip: Nylon does not stretch over time; therefore, it does not need to be stretched prior to using it in the construction of your jewelry projects.

D. Elastic Thread

Elastic thread is most commonly used in the construction of bracelets and is available in a variety of materials. In this book I encourage people to use a clear nylon product, such as Stretch Magic®. In my experience, this material is the most durable and does not lose its elasticity over time. Additionally, because of the nature of the nylon material, it allows you to easily string beads without the use of a needle.

E. Bead Tips

These metal components are used in the construction of threaded jewelry. Each consists of a small, cuplike base with a hole in the bottom and a hook attached to the rim of the base. You can tie a wire or string knot in the bead tip base and bend the hook part down to protect the knot. The bead tip hook can then be attached to a clasp.

F. French Wire

A fine, coiled metal tube, French wire is used to cover bead stringing materials. It is used near the clasp of a piece of jewelry to offer strength and durability and to give a professional finish to the piece.

G. Crimp Beads

These small, malleable, metal tubes are used to fasten stringing materials, such as flexible beading wire, nylon thread, and elastic thread. The metal tube can be flattened by flat-nose pliers or folded by crimping pliers, allowing it to be used as a clamp at the ends of a jewelry piece, near the clasp or at the other end.

C

POLYAMID | No. 4
Ø 0,60 mm

No

For stringing
pearls and beads

Polyamid Bead Cord

1 Nadel
needle fixed
2 meters

F

NATURAL SILK | No. 4
100% Naturseide | Ø 0,60 mm

stringing
nd beads

B

NATURAL SILK | No. 4
100% Naturseide | Ø 0,60 mm

D

For stringing
pearls and beads

E

A

G

PINPOINT PRECISION FOR JEWELRY, BEADING, HOBBIES, WATCH CRYSTALS, OPTICS, INDUSTRIAL APPLICATIONS

15245

ULTRA

A

C

E

B

D

Miscellaneous Items

A. Ruler

A measuring device is extremely useful when creating jewelry of a specific length. During the jewelry construction process, it is important to always have a ruler available (and calipers, to use when precise measurements in millimeters are necessary).

B. Glue

I recommend that you use a jewelry-specific glue for your projects, where applicable. G-S® Hypo Cement is the product I recommend, as it creates a tight bond without becoming brittle or discoloring over time.

C. Polishing Cloth

A polishing cloth is useful when working with metal jewelry. The cloth is coated with ultra-micro abrasive particles and luster agents, which add a beautiful shine to metal surfaces when used appropriately.

D. Abrasive Pad

An abrasive pad—such as Scotch-Brite®—is used to apply satin finishes to metal, without the use of heavy machinery.

E. Pen/Marker

A permanent marker, such as a Sharpie®, is useful when working with metal. It allows you to create patterns with precision and ensure specific measurements, prior to cutting piercing, or striking your material with a tool, such as a steel stamp or hammer.

F. Pearl Knotting Tweezers
*Not Shown

These tweezers help you place knots directly next to pearls. These tweezers do not have teeth on the inside, as many other types of tweezers do, so that your thread does not become frayed as you work with it.

BEGINNER JEWELRY TECHNIQUES

Before diving in to the series of projects ahead, it is important to explore some techniques in further detail. I recommend you use inexpensive materials while learning these techniques. This will ease any potential frustrations and lessen the waste of your better-quality materials. In this section, I'll discuss proper ways to manipulate your materials, demonstrate options for creating your jewelry, and address issues that may arise later. If you skip over this section, there will be a greater chance of frustration later on.

It is important when learning any new technique to meet challenges with patience. Careful practice will help you gain the skills needed to create beautiful, high-quality jewelry.

Finishing Ends for Beaded Projects

Option 1:

Crimping pliers
Wire cutters

Option 2:

Flat-nose pliers
Wire cutters

Option 3:

Flat-nose pliers
Wire cutters

Option 1:

Flexible beading wire, .014-inch
   diameter
Crimp tube beads, 2 mm
French wire, 0.7 mm
1 soldered jump ring, 5 mm

Option 2:

Flexible beading wire, .014-inch
   diameter
Crimp tube beads, 2 mm
Spring ring clasp, 6 mm

Option 3:

Flexible beading wire, .014-inch
   diameter
Crimp tube beads, 2 mm
Lobster clasp, 6 mm
French wire, 0.7 mm

This section presents three techniques for finishing jewelry at the ends using a flexible beading wire material. See the individual projects in the Bead Stringing section on pages 50–77 for further information.

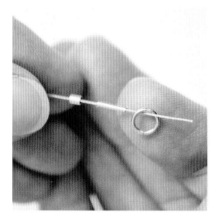

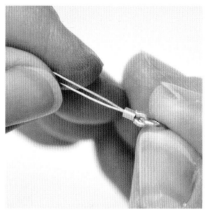

Step 1

String one crimp bead, one small piece of French wire, and one jump ring over the end of the flexible beading wire.

You may also begin the project with a clasp instead of jump ring, as shown in Options 2 and 3.

Step 2

Bring the wire back through the top of the crimp bead, creating a loop for the jump ring. Position the French wire evenly through the jump ring, as shown.

Step 3

Slide the crimp bead close to the jump ring, removing most of the slack from the loop. The length of the French wire will determine the size of the loop you are able to create.

Step 7

Place the crimp bead inside the crimping pliers again, this time at station 2. The dent in your crimp should be facing up, toward the tip of the pliers. Squeeze the handles on the pliers to fold the crimp bead closed.

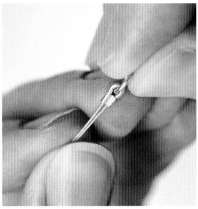

Step 4

Become familiar with the crimping pliers. You will notice there are two notches, or "stations," in the jaws. The station closest to the handles is station 1. The station closest to the tip is station 2.

Step 5

Place the crimp bead centered in station 1 and squeeze the handles of the pliers.

Step 6

After completing step 5 you will notice that the crimp bead now has a dent that runs down the center of the bead.

8

Step 8

The jump ring is now secure on the wire. The crimp is now smaller in appearance and has kept its cylindrical shape. This is my preferred method for closing crimp beads because it has a lower profile than other methods and doesn't create sharp corners on the crimp bead. You can either trim the wire tail with flush wire cutters or place both wires inside the holes of the beads used in your project.

Note: To complete a project, repeat the crimping process on the other end with a clasp instead of a soldered jump ring.

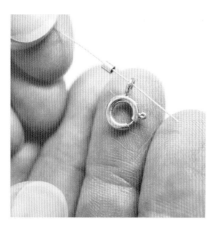

Step 1

String one crimp bead and clasp over the end of the flexible beading wire.

Step 2

Bring the wire back through the crimp bead, creating a loop for your clasp.

Step 3

Slide the crimp bead close to the clasp, removing most of the slack from the loop. It is helpful to leave a small amount of space in the loop so that the clasp has some mobility.

Note: To complete a project, repeat the crimping process on the other end with a soldered jump ring instead of the clasp.

Step 4

Place the crimp bead between the jaws of the flat-nose pliers, and flatten the crimp completely by squeezing the handles of the pliers.

Step 5

The clasp is now secure on the wire and the crimp is a flat square. You can either trim the small piece of wire at the bottom of the crimp with flush wire cutters or place both pieces of wire inside the holes of the beads used in your project.

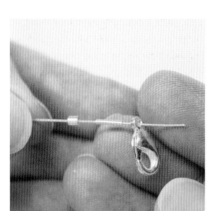

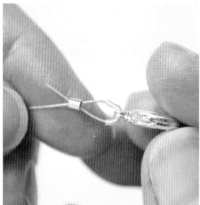

Step 1

String one crimp bead, one small piece of French wire of matching color to the clasp, and the clasp over the end of the flexible beading wire.

Step 2

Bring the wire back through the top of the crimp bead, creating a loop for the clasp. Position the French wire evenly through the loop in the clasp, as shown.

Step 3

Slide the crimp bead close to the clasp, removing most of the slack from the loop. The length of the French wire will determine the size of the loop you are able to create.

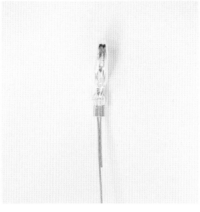

Note: To complete a project, repeat the crimping process on the other end with a soldered jump ring instead of the clasp.

Step 4

Place the crimp bead between the jaws of flat-nose pliers and flatten the crimp bead completely by squeezing the plier handles.

Step 5

The clasp is now secure on the wire and the crimp bead is a flat square. The French wire matches the color of your clasp and hides the color of the beading wire, giving your jewelry a more polished look. You can either trim the wire tail flush with the bottom of the crimp bead with wire cutters or place both wires inside the holes of the beads used in your project.

Wire Wrapping

Flat-nose pliers
Round-nose pliers
Wire cutters

3 inches (7.6 cm) wire, 22-gauge
Bead

Wire wrapping is an important skill in jewelry making because it allows you to assemble jewelry without the need for extensive tools, such as torches, hammers, and drills. By mastering the technique of wire wrapping, you can create professional-quality jewelry that has durability for years to come.

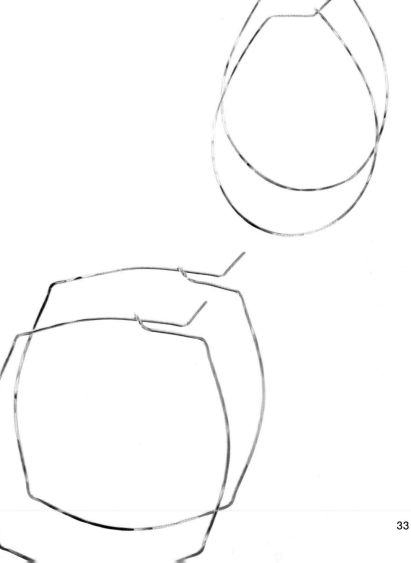

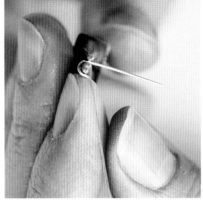

Step 1

Make a 90-degree bend in your wire, 1 inch (2.5 cm) from the top. To properly execute this step, pinch your wire with round-nose pliers where you want to make your bend. Either roll your pliers 90 degrees or use your fingers to manipulate the wire over the tip of your pliers, making a 90-degree bend.

Step 2

Create a question mark shape in your wire using round-nose pliers. Pinch your wire approximately ⅛ inch (3 mm) from the bend you created, on the shorter end of the wire. Either roll your pliers back toward your original bend or use your fingers to pull the short piece of wire over the tip of the pliers, creating a question mark shape.

Step 3

Create a full circle from the question mark shape. The best way to do this is by placing one tip of the pliers inside the loop and pinching the pliers in place. Using your fingers, pull the wire tail in the direction of the loop, creating a full circle, as shown.

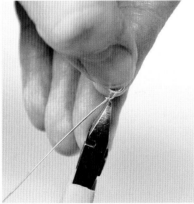

Step 7

Place the flush side of the wire cutters against your wire wrap and cut the small piece of wire so the remaining part is flush with the wrap. Leave the long piece of wire that extends straight out from the bottom of the loop to later apply your bead of choice.

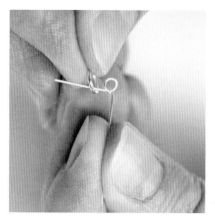  

Step 4

If you are attaching anything to your loop, simply slide it over the wire tail until it nestles inside the loop. If you are closing the loop without attaching something, you can skip to step 5.

Step 5

Whether you have attached something to your loop or not, you will execute this step in the same way. Using round-nose pliers, pinch your loop with the jaws of the pliers, perpendicular to the loop, as shown. This will hold the shape of your circle as you wrap the loop closed.

Step 6

While holding the loop as shown in step 5, use flat-nose pliers to wrap the tail piece of wire around the base of the loop. You can wrap your wire as many times as you desire, but only one wrap is necessary to securely complete your loop.

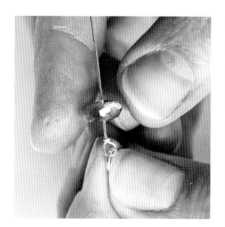

Step 8

Attach a bead to the 2-inch (5 cm) piece of wire that extends from your loop. At this point you will repeat steps 1–7 (excluding step 4 if you are not attaching anything) to create a loop on the opposite side of your bead. Pinch your wire directly against the bead with round-nose pliers prior to creating a bend like the bend in step 1.

Pearl Knotting

Option 2:

Knotting tweezers

Option 1:

Silk thread with
    needle attached, size 4
Drilled pearls, 6 mm

Option 2:

Silk thread with needle attached,
    size 4
Drilled pearls, 6 mm

This section presents technique options for how to successfully place and tighten knots between pearls. For more information on knotting, including attaching a clasp, see the individual projects in the Projects section.

1

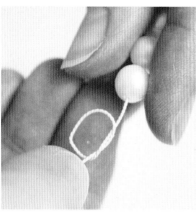

2

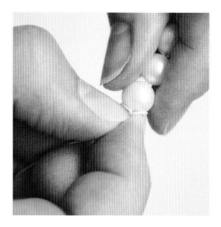

3

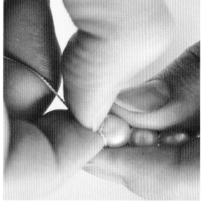

Step 1

Tie an overhand knot close to the pearl. It is best to place the knot as close to the pearl as possible so you can successfully tighten the thread and place the knot in the appropriate position.

Step 2

Place your thumb and index finger on either side of the knot, next to the pearl. Hold the remaining thread by making a fist with the remaining three fingers on the same hand, as shown.

Step 3

Keeping a tight grip on the thread with the back three fingers, begin to tighten the knot.

7

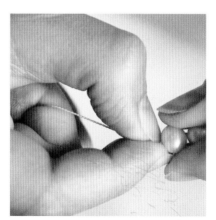

Step 7

Again, pull the slack from the knot by making a fist with the back three fingers while extending your thumb and forefinger. It is helpful, as the knot becomes tight, to hold the knot in place with your thumbnail.

 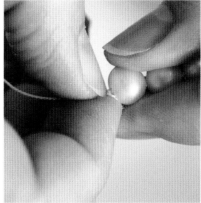 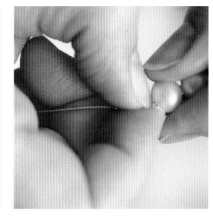

Step 4

As you tighten your fist, keep your thumb and forefinger in place so that the knot is positioned next to the pearl. The easiest way to accomplish this is by pulling the thread with the back three fingers while extending the thumb and forefinger.

Step 5

Loosen your grip on the thread while holding the thumb and forefinger in place.

Step 6

Reposition the back three fingers and repeat step 3.

Step 8

Once the knot is complete, place your thumbnail next to your knot and remove any remaining slack from the knot by pulling the thread.

1

2

3

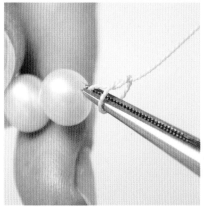

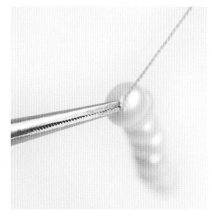

Step 1

Tie an overhand knot close to the pearl. It is best to place the knot as close to the pearl as possible so you can successfully tighten the thread and place the knot appropriately.

Step 2

Using a set of knotting tweezers (shown above), place the tips of the tweezers through the loop in the knot and pinch the thread next to the pearl where you want the completed knot to be positioned.

Step 3

While holding the tweezers in place, tighten the knot by pulling the thread and sliding the knot down the tips of the tweezers.

Tip: Although Option 2 appears to be the easier option, I highly recommend practicing and mastering the skills shown in Option 1. You will find that incorporating a tool greatly slows the speed at which you can place knots in their proper position.

Step 4

Remove the tweezers from the knot and place them perpendicular to the thread, just above the knot you have just created. Pull the thread while holding the tweezers in place to remove any remaining slack from the knot.

Opening & Closing Jump Rings

The function of this section is to explain the proper way to open and close jump rings. Jump rings are used often in jewelry construction, and it will benefit you to know how to use them properly in your jewelry items.

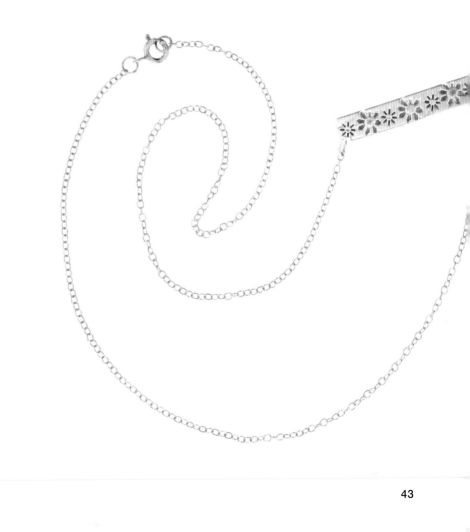

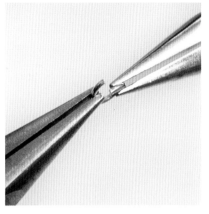
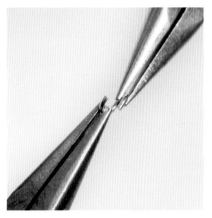

Step 1

Locate the opening in the jump ring. Grasp one pair of flat-nose pliers in each hand and place the tips of the pliers on either side of the jump ring opening.

Step 2

Begin opening the jump ring by twisting one side toward you and the other side away from you.

Step 3

Continue opening the jump ring until the gap in the jump ring is large enough to attach the ring to your item of choice. Be careful not to open the jump ring too wide, as this can distort or break it.

Step 4

Once the jump ring is opened appropriately, attach your item of choice.

Step 5

Again, grasping one pair of flat-nose pliers in each hand, place the tips of the pliers on either side of the jump ring opening. Begin twisting the jump ring closed, reversing the directions from step 2.

Step 6

Continue twisting both sides of the jump ring until the ends match up and the gap has been closed.

Hammering Metal

Goldsmith hammer
and/or chasing hammer

Metal sheet and/or wire

Metal forging dates back to early history and is still widely used today in many professions. Striking metal between a hammer and a steel surface allows you to create beautiful shapes and designs.

When working with metal, it is important to become familiar with the term *work-hardening*, which describes the strength or hardness of a metal, and is determined by how the metal has been manipulated. When metal is heated, the process is called "annealing." The molecules of the metal become separated, creating a softer and more malleable material. When tension, compression, or torsion is applied to metal (hammering is one example), the crystal formation is moved closer together, creating a stiffer, more rigid material. By understanding this concept you will know how to easily form metal, depending on its state of hardness. For example, if your wire is stiff and feels brittle as you attempt to bend it, then you will want to heat the metal, preferably with a torch, to make the metal softer and less brittle as you work with it.

I encourage you to research the topic of metal forging further, as this only scratches the surface of this technique. Forging lets you create unique jewelry with the utmost strength and durability.

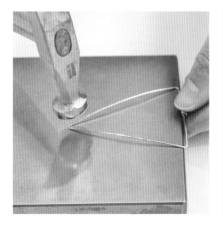
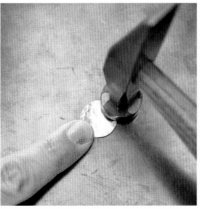

PROJECTS

The projects I have selected for this book are designed to help you move through a series of instructions, ranging from easy to moderately difficult, for beginners. These projects will help you learn a wide range of techniques, without formal education. All of these projects can be constructed in the comfort of your home, and the tools and materials can be found at your local bead or craft store. It is my hope that you use these projects to learn specific techniques for future designs. As my mother always said, "Practice makes perfect." The more you practice the techniques in this book, the faster and more precisely you will be able to execute them. Have fun making these projects and share what you have learned with others.

Tip: Always take time to properly set up your work station. Clear away any unnecessary items, choose a space with good lighting, and have all of your tools and materials ready to go. This will reduce the amount of time needed to complete your projects and avoid any added frustrations.

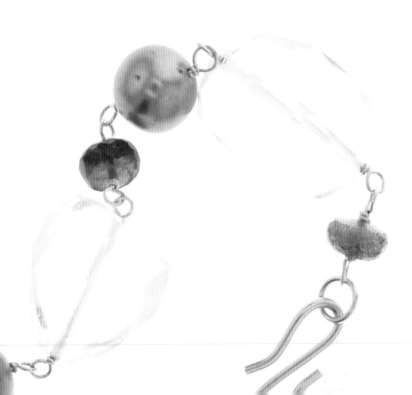

Flexible Beading Wire Bracelet

Ruby
chalcedony

Softflex
wire

14K gold-filled
bar

Spring ring
clasp

Tools

Flush wire cutters
Crimping pliers *Optional
Flat-nose pliers

Materials

9 inches (23 cm) of of flexible
    beading wire, .014-inch diameter
½ inch (1.3 cm) French
    wire *Optional
2 tube crimp beads, 2 mm
Spring ring clasp, 5 mm
1 soldered jump ring
Heart-shaped stone briolettes, 8 mm
1½-inch (3.8 cm) curved tube bead
4 to 5 inches (10 to 12.5 cm) of beads
Jump ring, 5 mm

Helpful Items

Ruler

In this project we will explore the use of flexible beading wire when constructing jewelry, as well as examine options for attaching clasps. Flexible beading wire provides endless design possibilities while assuring the durability and longevity of your jewelry.

Note: To measure your wrist, simply drape a string around your wrist until the ends meet. Mark that spot on your string and then measure the length of the string on a ruler to get a precise measurement.

SETTING UP

Cut a 9-inch (23 cm) piece of flexible beading wire. The standard bracelet length is 7 inches (17 cm). You will need the additional 1 inch (2.5 cm) on either end to finish your bracelet at the clasp. If desired, cut two pieces of French wire, ¹/₄ inch (6 mm) each. Have a ruler handy and all necessary tools and beads ready.

Step 1

String one crimp bead and one piece of French wire over the end of flexible beading wire.

Note: I prefer to use French wire to hide the flexible beading wire around my clasp. French wire comes in silver and gold metals, so it is easy to keep your metal colors consistent with your clasp, which keeps the steel color of the flexible beading wire from being visible. It also gives your jewelry a more polished look. You can choose to omit this material from your project and simply start with just the crimp bead.

Step 2

String one clasp of your choice over the end of flexible beading wire. Create a loop with the flexible beading wire wire by placing the end back through the crimp bead, leaving the clasp hanging from the loop you have created.

Step 3

Pull the wire tight through the crimp bead until the French wire is snug around the loop of the clasp. If you are not using French wire, still pull the wire tight until nearly all slack is removed from the loop.

Step 4

Become familiar with the crimping pliers. You will notice there are two notches, or "stations," in the tips. The station closest to the handles is station 1. The station closest to the tip is station 2.

Note: I prefer crimping pliers because it creates a lower profile on your crimp beads and eliminates any possible sharp edges. You can use flat-nose pliers in place of crimping pliers. To do so, simply squeeze your crimp bead with your flat-nose pliers until your crimp bead is completely flat. This will create more of a square shape to your crimp bead once flattened. If you are using this method, you can skip to step 8. See pages 24–31 in the Beginner Jewelry Techniques section for additional options.

Step 5

Place the crimp bead inside station 1. Squeeze the pliers and crease the crimp down the center.

Step 6

Rotate the crimp bead 90 degrees so that the crease is facing upward. Move the crimp bead to station 2 and squeeze the pliers, folding the crimp bead in half.

 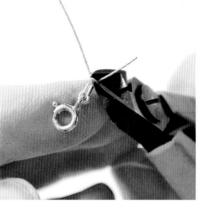 

Step 7

Use a pair of flat-nose pliers to close the crimp bead completely, by gently squeezing the crimp on its flat sides.

Step 8

Remove the short piece of wire using the flush side of your wire cutters. If the bead holes are large enough, you may consider keeping this short piece attached and sliding your beads over both pieces of wire.

Step 9

Begin stringing your beads on the wire. Keep in mind which direction you want your beads to be facing. This is particularly important if you are following a specific design or pattern.

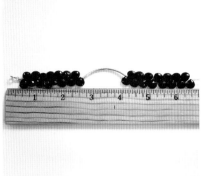

Step 10

Track the length as you work. Depending on the size of your wrist, you might choose to have the final length slightly smaller or larger than the standard wrist measurement of 7 inches (18 cm). If you have a centerpiece for your bracelet, such as the curved tube bead in this project, use a ruler to mark your progress so it is placed appropriately.

Step 11

Complete the second half of your bracelet, taking note of your final measurement and the placement of beads, to achieve your desired design.

Step 12

String a crimp bead and a piece of French wire* onto the end of your wire.

*See the note in step 1 if you are choosing to omit the French wire.

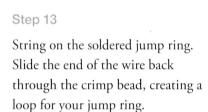

Step 13

String on the soldered jump ring. Slide the end of the wire back through the crimp bead, creating a loop for your jump ring.

Step 14

Remove the slack from the loop by pulling the end of wire through the crimp bead. Pull the wire until the French wire is snug around the jump ring.

Tip: If your bead holes are large enough, you can consider stringing the wire through the last three or four beads, before pulling it tight. This will add extra strength and security to your finished piece.

Step 15

Place the crimp bead inside station 1 of the crimping pliers. Squeeze the pliers to crease the crimp down the center.

Step 16

Rotate the crimp 90 degrees so that the crease is facing upward. Move the crimp to station 2 and squeeze the pliers, folding the crimp bead in half. Again, you can use flat-nose pliers to give the crimp an additional squeeze to ensure complete closure.

Step 17

Remove the wire tail using the flush side of the wire cutters. If you chose to string the wire end through the last three or four beads, cut the wire as close to that last bead as possible.

Your bracelet is now complete! You have successfully executed a simple yet widely used method for creating beaded jewelry. You can now apply this technique to a wide variety of jewelry designs, such as single and multi-strand bracelets and necklaces.

elastic cord

glass beads

Sugilite stones.

Elastic Beaded Bracelet

Flush wire cutters
Flat-nose pliers

9 inches (23 cm) clear
   elastic stringing material, 0.5 mm
1 tube crimp bead
3 stone nugget beads, 15 × 30 mm
18 faceted glass rondelle beads,
   6 mm

Masking tape *Optional
Ruler

In this project I use a crimp bead to finish and close the elastic. There is also the method of simply tying the ends together in a knot, but I find this method is not as secure as using a crimp bead. If you do not find the crimp bead aesthetically pleasing, you can use the knot method.

SETTING UP

Cut a 9-inch (23 cm) piece of elastic stringing material. The standard bracelet length is 7 inches (18 cm). You will need the additional inch (2.5 cm) on either end to finish your bracelet at the crimp or knot.

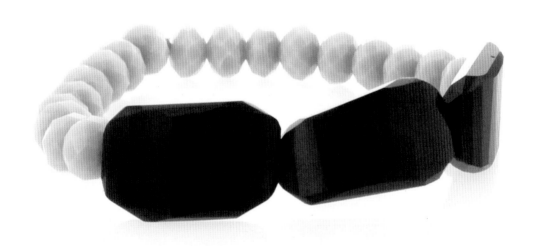

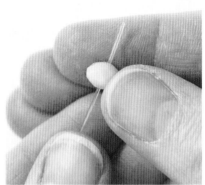

Step 1

Tie an overhand knot in the end of the elastic. You may also use a small piece of tape in place of a knot. String a crimp bead onto the end of the elastic and slide it down toward the knot or tape.

Tip: Note the size of the hole in your crimp bead. It will need to be large enough for your elastic thread to be doubled inside.

Step 2

Begin stringing your beads onto the elastic. Keep in mind which way you want your beads to face. This is particularly important if there is a specific design or pattern to your bracelet.

Step 3

Track the length as you work. Depending on the size of your wrist, you might choose to have the final length slightly smaller or larger than the standard wrist measurement of 7 inches (18 cm). If you have a centerpiece for your bracelet, use a ruler to mark your progress so that it is placed appropriately.

  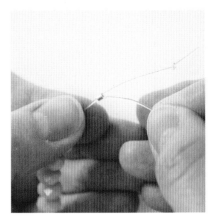

Step 4

Complete the second half of your bracelet, working toward your desired final length.

Step 5

Use a ruler to take note of your final measurement and placement of beads prior to moving on to the next step.

Step 6

String the second end of your elastic through the crimp bead, passing through in the opposite direction from the way the bead was put on.

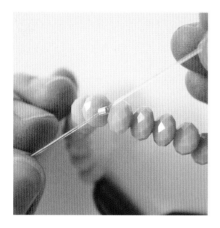 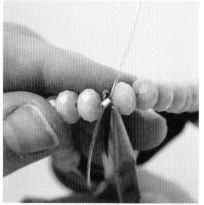 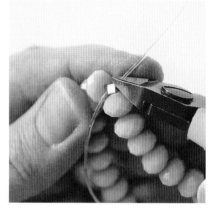

Step 7

Pull both ends of the elastic until the crimp bead is tight between your beads.

Tip: Do not pull the elastic any farther than what is necessary to remove slack. If you pull beyond this point, you are removing the range of elasticity and your bracelet has a greater chance of breaking.

Step 8

Using flat-nose pliers, squeeze the crimp bead. The crimp should now be a flat square. Do not close the crimp more than necessary, as the elastic has a greater chance of being severed if you do.

Note: I prefer to use flat-nose pliers for elastic bracelets rather than crimping pliers. I find that, due to the thickness of the elastic, crimping pliers squeeze the crimp too tightly and the elastic can be severed.

Step 9

Trim the elastic tails using the flush side of the wire cutters. I do not recommend threading your elastic through the beads near the crimp, because those tail pieces of elastic will come out of the beads as you stretch your bracelet on and off your wrist. It is best to trim the elastic next to the crimp bead.

Congratulations on successfully completing your elastic bracelet! You can now apply this technique to countless projects, creating beautifully stacked bracelets that can be worn and shared with others. Elastic bracelets can be created on a very small budget, and they make wonderful gifts!

Multi-strand Bracelet

crimped w/ softflex *french wire*

~Natural stones

Toggle clasp

Flush wire cutters
Flat-nose pliers
Crimping pliers *Optional

28 inches (71.6 cm) flexible
   beading wire, .014 diameter
2 soldered jump rings, 10 mm
1 toggle clasp
6 tube crimp beads, 2 mm
1½ inches (3.8 cm) French wire,
   0.7 mm *Optional
21 inches (53.5 cm) of faceted
   rondelle stone beads, 4 mm
2 unsoldered jump rings, 6 mm

Ruler
Masking tape

Learning how to properly assemble multi-strand jewelry, as in this brace-let project, will allow you to expand your jewelry designs and execute a clean finish with greater durability.

SETTING UP

Cut 3 pieces of wire, each 9¼ inches (23.5 cm) in length. The standard bracelet length is 7 inches (18 cm), but bracelets with multiple strands often have a tighter fit. I recommend a finished length of 7¼ inches (18.4 cm) for this project. Be sure to account for the length of the clasp and deduct that measurement when determining the length of your beaded strands. You will need an additional inch (2.5 cm) on either end of each piece of flexible beading wire to finish your bracelet at the clasp. Cut six pieces of French wire, ¼ inch (6 mm) each. Have a ruler handy and all necessary tools and beads ready. Working in a clean and organized work space is always recommended.

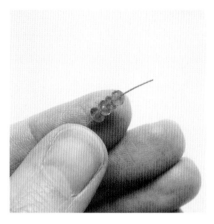

Step 1

See pages 42–45 for further instructions on attaching jump rings. Attach a large jump ring to the circle half of the toggle clasp. Review the available options for attaching flexible beading wire with crimp beads in the Beginner Jewelry Techniques section, on pages 24–31. Once you have selected your desired method (I am using Option 3, shown on pages 30–31), attach each of the three pieces of wire to the large jump ring, as shown.

Step 2

Using the flush side of the wire cutters, remove the wire tails from each strand, cutting next to the crimp beads.

Step 3

Begin stringing your beads onto one of the wires. When creating jewelry with multiple strands, I find it helpful to string all strands simultaneously, in 1-inch (2.5 cm) sections. This helps to keep the pattern consistent.

  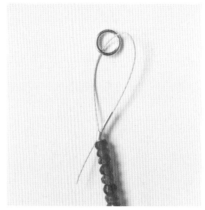

Step 4

Track your progress as you work. This is particularly important in multi-strand jewelry. Each strand must be consistent in length, or the jewelry will not lie properly when worn.

Step 5

Continue stringing each strand until you have reached your desired length. The standard bracelet length is 7 inches (18 cm), but bracelets with multiple strands often have a tighter fit. I recommend a finished length of 7¼ inches (18.4 cm) for this project. Be sure to account for the length of the clasp and deduct that measurement when determining the length of your beaded strands.

Step 6

Begin attaching each strand to a second large jump ring, using the same method you used in step 1. Again, you can reference pages 24–31 for details. Be careful not to accidentally remove the beads from the other two strands as you attach the first strand. It is helpful to place a small amount of tape on the ends of the other two strands while you work.

Step 7

Repeat step 6 with the second strand, after strand 1 is secured and the crimp bead is properly crimped.

Step 8

When working with the second and third strands, it is helpful to allow a small amount of space between strands as you tighten the wire. This will provide you with the necessary space to properly secure each crimp bead as you work.

Step 9

Repeat step 6 one final time with the third strand.

Step 10

After all three strands are securely attached, and all the wire tails have been properly trimmed, begin setting up the clasp. Attach one small jump ring to the T-bar half of the clasp.

Step 11

Attach the T-bar and jump ring to the bracelet using an additional small jump ring, as shown.

Step 12

After you have securely attached the T-bar to your bracelet, test the functionality of the toggle. If you find the T-bar does not easily slide through the circle half of the clasp, you may want to add one additional small jump ring to the T-bar. This will allow extra mobility for the T-bar to fit through the circle.

Congratulations on the completion of your first multi-strand bracelet! You may have found this project to be challenging at times, but with practice and a deeper understanding of the materials and process, this technique can be a fun and rewarding method of creating stunning jewelry.

Beaded Necklace on Silk

Tools

Flush wire cutters
Flat-nose pliers
Round-nose pliers

Materials

Silk thread with needle attached,
    size 4
2 bead tips, 3 mm
1 spring ring clasp, 5 mm
8 inches (20 cm) of faceted teardrop
    stone beads, 10 × 16 mm
8 inches (20 cm) of faceted rondelle
    stone beads, 6 mm
1 unsoldered jump ring, 6 mm

Helpful
Items

Ruler
Jeweler's tweezers
Jeweler's glue

In previous projects in this book, we have explored several options for stringing beads and stones when creating jewelry. In this project, silk beading thread provides a fluidity for wearable pieces that is unmatched by any other material. Although this is not the most durable option, it is my favorite.

SETTING UP

Before beginning your project, be sure to have all tools and materials ready. It is helpful to have a clean work space, clear of clutter and with proper lighting. This will make the process smoother and faster, and your materials won't get lost or misplaced.

Tip: It is important to purchase silk or nylon thread with the needle attached. The silk product shown on the opposite page is offered in a variety of colors and thread sizes. Pay attention to the size of the holes in your beads and be sure to get the correct thread size. You can also purchase this product in a nylon material. If you are using nylon you do not need to stretch your thread, as called for in step 1.

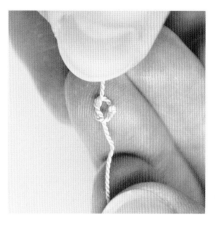

Step 1

Remove the entire thread from the card. Begin at one end of the thread and stretch the silk in small sections, working toward the opposite end. This is a very important step. If you don't pre-stretch the silk before stringing your necklace, the weight of the beads will cause the silk to stretch over time, creating gaps in your jewelry. If you are using a nylon material, you can begin at step 2.

Step 2

Tie a single overhand knot near the end of the thread opposite the needle. Pull the knot tight.

Step 3

Create a double overhand knot by tying a second knot directly over the first. Pull the knot tight.

 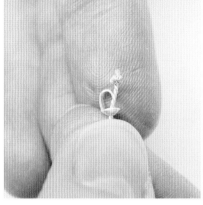 

Step 4

Trim the thread tail. Do not trim too close to the knot, or it could come untied.

Step 5

String one of the bead tips onto the thread by placing the needle through the hole on the inside of the bead tip base. If you have done this properly, the hook on the bead tip should face away from the long piece of thread, and the knot you created should nestle inside the bead tip base, as shown.

Step 6

Attach the clasp to the hook of the bead tip. Using a pair of flat-nose pliers, gently squeeze the top of the hook and the bottom side of the cup to close the hook toward the base. Be sure to squeeze until the end of the hook reaches the base, completely closing any gaps.

Tip: The hooks on bead tips can be brittle. Squeeze gently to avoid breaking them.

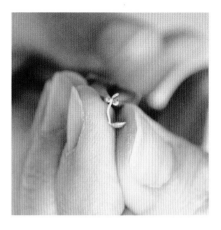

Step 7

Begin stringing your beads. Do not force beads onto the thread if the holes are too small. This could cause the needle to break away from the thread.

Step 8

Mark your progress with a ruler as you work. This is particularly helpful when attempting to create a symmetrical pattern. See page 169 for a chart on necklace lengths.

Step 9

Once you have reached the desired length of your necklace, prepare the second bead tip. Using round-nose pliers, gently open the hook. This will give you the space needed to tie a double knot inside the bead tip base.

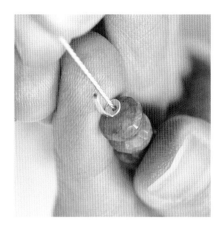  

Step 10

String the bead tip onto the thread by placing the needle through the hole in the bottom of the base. The hook on your bead tip should be facing away from your beads, as shown.

Step 11

Pull the thread taut while pushing the beads against the opposite end of the clasp, to remove any slack from the thread prior to completing your knot. This will allow the knot to nestle inside the bead tip base once the beads on the thread are released. Tie a single overhand knot. Tighten the knot inside the base of the bead tip.

Step 12

Create a double overhand knot. It is important to loop the thread around the base of the first knot before you pull the second knot tight. This will help you position your knots farther inside the bead tip base, once the knot is tightened.

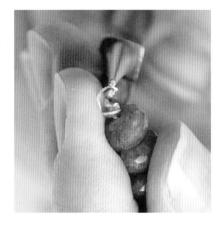

Step 13

Using your thumbnail or a pair of tweezers, pull any remaining slack from your knots. This will position the knot properly and add extra security to your necklace.

Step 14

Trim the thread by placing the flush side of the wire cutters against the knot. Do not trim the thread too close to the knot.

Step 15

Using round-nose pliers, gently re-form the hook in the bead tip. Be sure to leave an opening in the hook and do not close the bead tip at this time.

Step 16

Place a jump ring in the hook.

Step 17

Again, using a pair of flat-nose pliers, gently squeeze the top of the hook and the bottom of the cup to close the hook.

Tip: It is helpful at this stage to apply a small amount of jeweler's glue to the inside of the bead tip bases for extra security. Do not apply too much glue, or you'll create a mess.

Congratulations on completing your necklace! There are many ways to make threaded jewelry, but this method is my favorite. It provides durability as well as a clean and polished look. This technique will become easier with practice, and I encourage you to have patience. Using thread in jewelry construction offers a softness and fluidity that no other material can match.

Herkimer diamonds

spikes

Simple Wire Earrings

Flush wire cutters
Round-nose pliers
Flat-nose pliers

6 inches (15 cm) wire, 22-gauge
2 spike embellishments, 1½ inches
    (3.8 cm) long
2 faceted stone beads, 15 mm
1 pair of ear wires

The following project showcases a widely used technique in jewelry making. Wire wrapping is a very versatile skill that will allow you to create a large variety of designs, including, but not limited to, earrings, necklaces, and bracelets. In this project, we execute an edgy pair of earrings that can be created quickly and on a minimal budget.

SETTING UP

Prior to beginning your project, have all tools and materials ready. Have a clean work space, clear of clutter and with proper lighting. This will make the process smoother and faster, and your materials won't get lost or misplaced.

 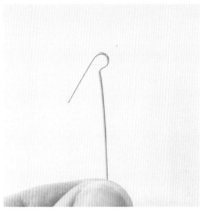 

Step 1

With wire cutters, cut the wire in half. Using round-nose pliers, make a 90-degree bend in one of the 3-inch (7.6 cm) pieces of wire, 1 inch (2.5 cm) from the end.

Step 2

Using round-nose pliers again, create a question mark shape past the bend you just created. See page 34 in the Beginner Jewelry Techniques section for more detailed instructions on this step.

Step 3

Create a full circle by placing the one tip of the round-nose pliers inside the question mark and pulling the short piece of wire around the bottom of the pliers' tips.

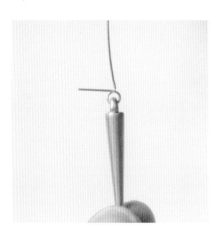  

Step 4

Add your embellishment by sliding it onto the short end of the wire and nestling it inside the loop.

Step 5

Wrap the wire tail around the long piece of wire. See pages 32–35 for additional details on wire wrapping techniques.

Step 6

Trim the wire tail by using the flush side of the wire cutters.

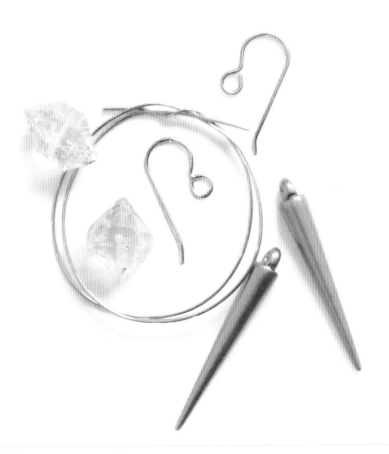

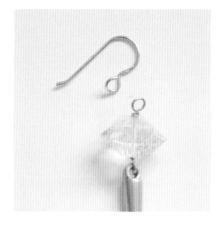

Step 7

Add a bead to the long piece of wire. Using round-nose pliers, pinch the wire at the top of the bead to create a 90-degree angle.

Tip: It is important to pinch the wire at the top of the bead BEFORE bending the wire. This will create the small space between your bead and the 90-degree angle needed to wrap the loop.

Step 8

Repeat step 5 to complete the loop.

Step 9

Using flat-nose pliers, gently open the loop on the ear wire, similar to how you would open a jump ring by twisting it (see page 44). Do not open the loop by pulling it straight out. This will deform the loop and make it difficult to close.

Step 10

Attach the dangle to the ear wire.
Using flat-nose pliers, close the
loop on the ear wire until there are
no gaps.

You have successfully completed your wire-wrapped earrings! This is a
simple technique that can be used in many facets of jewelry design. Being
able to manipulate and attach stones and beads provides endless possibilities. This is a simple and cost-effective way to make jewelry that has
structural integrity and can last for years to come.

curved tube frame

flat cable chain

Chandelier
Earrings

Tools

Flush wire cutters
Flat-nose pliers
Round-nose pliers

Materials

10 inches (25 cm) wire, 22-gauge
7 inches (18 cm) flat cable chain,
    2.5 mm
2 curved tube beads, 1¼ inches
    (3 cm) long, 3 mm diameter
1 pair of ear wires

Helpful
Items

Ruler

In this project, the steps instruct you to create one earring at a time. If you prefer to make both earrings simultaneously, you will begin with two pieces of 22-gauge wire 5 inches (12.7 cm) long and apply all instructions to both pieces before proceeding to the next step. The continuity of making both earrings simultaneously can help to ensure each piece is identical to the other.

SETTING UP

Prior to beginning your project, have all tools and materials ready. It is helpful to have a clean work space that is clear of clutter and has proper lighting. This will make the process smoother and faster, and your materials won't get lost or misplaced.

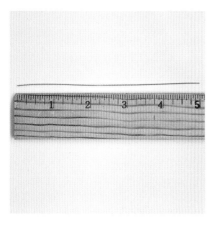 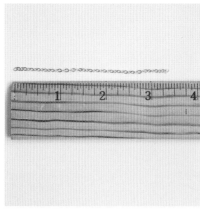 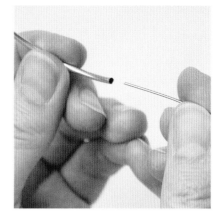

Step 1

Cut 5 inches (12.7 cm) of 22-gauge wire using the flush side of the wire cutters.

Step 2

Cut 3½ inches (9 cm) of cable chain. Remove any severed links on the ends of the chain.

Step 3

Slide one of the curved tube beads onto the wire until the tubing is centered.

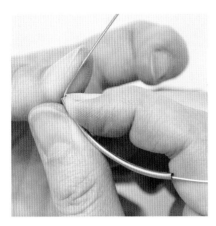  

Step 4

Create a sharp bend on the wire where it meets one end of the tubing. You can use flat-nose pliers to assist you in the process.

Tip: Tubing can be creased and dented easily. To keep the end of your tubing from splitting, place your thumbnail or a pair of flat-nose pliers next to the opening in the tubing so it does not become damaged in the bending process.

Step 5

Repeat step 4 on the opposite side of the tubing. Manipulate both pieces of wire until they are symmetrical.

Step 6

Attach the chain to your earring frame by sliding one end of the wire through the end link on one side of the chain. Attach the other end of the chain to the other end of the wire in the same way. Be mindful of how you slide the chain on, avoiding any twists in the chain.

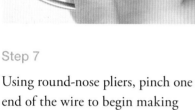

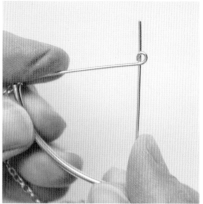

Step 7

Using round-nose pliers, pinch one end of the wire to begin making the loop.

Step 8

While keeping a tight grip with the pliers, roll your wrist to create a loop in the wire, using your other hand for resistance to avoid any additional bends in the wire frame. The loop should be formed so your earring will face forward once attached to the ear wire. Take note of the direction of the loop on your ear wire and create the loop in your earring frame so it will hang perpendicular to the loop wire. (See the photo of the finished project on page 85 for guidance.)

Step 9

Bring both sides of wire on your frame together until they overlap just below the loop.

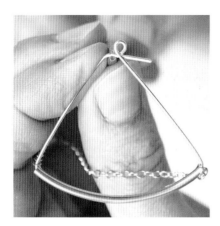

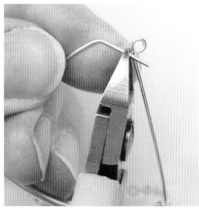

Step 10

Mark your wire, equal to the distance from the tube to the bottom of the loop on the opposite side of the wire, and create a bend, moving it toward the loop as shown.

Step 11

Trim the wire tail ¼ inch (6 mm) from the bend, using the flush side of the wire cutters.

Step 12

Using flat-nose pliers, pinch the end of the wire and roll your wrist toward the loop to make a loop that will be perpendicular to the loop on the other end (see step 13 for guidance), but don't close the loop yet.

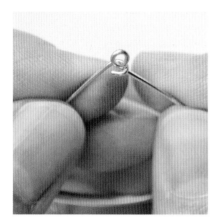

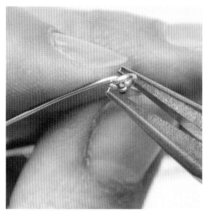

Step 13

Hook the wire around the your frame, just beneath your original loop.

Step 14

Using flat-nose pliers, pinch the second loop closed. The tighter you close the loop around your frame, the more durable it will be.

Step 15

Open the loop of the ear wire. Twist the loop open, rather than pulling it straight out. This will help maintain the original shape of the loop in your ear wire once it is closed.

You have successfully completed your chandelier earrings! If you have trouble finding the exact tubing used in this project, consider using smaller beads that line up in the center to add a pop of color and texture. Larger earring designs are a fun and cost-effective way to create stunning accessories for any outfit.

Step 16

Attach the earring frame to the loop of the ear wire. Using flat-nose pliers, twist the ear wire loop closed completely. Repeat step 1–16 to create a second earring.

Handmade clasp

Large quartz stones —

wire wrapped construction

Natural pearl — Labradorite

Linked Bracelet

Tools

Flush wire cutters
Round-nose pliers
Flat-nose pliers

Materials

Approximately 30 inches (76 cm)
   wire, 24-gauge
1 clasp (see pages 108–113 for
   instructions on making the
   clasp shown in this project)
2 soldered jump rings, 10 mm
3 drilled pearls, 11 mm
4 faceted rondelle stone beads, 6 mm
3 faceted stone beads, 15 × 20 mm

In this project we use the same wire wrapping technique as discussed on pages 32–35. We will build upon that technique to better understand how to create linked jewelry by assembling designs using wire and minimal tools.

SETTING UP

Prior to beginning your project, have all tools and materials ready. It is helpful to have a clean work space, clear of clutter and with proper lighting. Once your work space is properly set up, measure the size of your beads and pearls. With the flush side of the wire cutters, cut a piece of wire for each of your beads and pearls, leaving a minimum of 1 inch (2.5 cm) on each end of the wire. The wire will pass through the bead or pearl and you will make a connecting loop on each end to attach to the next component, which is why you need the extra length of wire on each end. For example, if your bead is ½ inch (12 mm) in size, your wire length will be 2½ to 3 inches (6.4 to 7.6 cm).

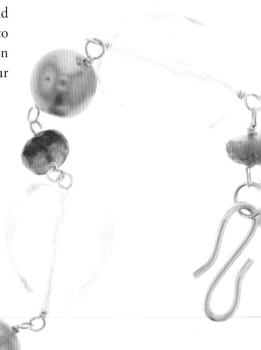

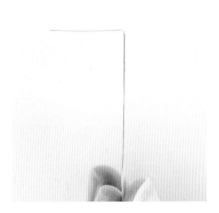  

Step 1

Using round-nose pliers, make a 90-degree bend in one of the 3-inch (7.6 cm) pieces of wire, or in whatever length of wire you need for your bead, 1 inch (2.5 cm) from the end.

Step 2

Using round-nose pliers again, create a question mark shape past the bend you just created. See page 34 in the Beginner Jewelry Techniques section for more detailed instructions on this step.

Step 3

Create a full circle with the wire tail by placing the round-nose pliers inside the question mark and pulling the tail around the bottom of the pliers' tips.

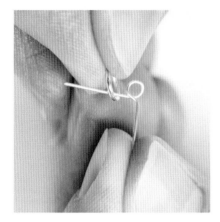  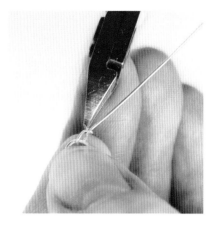

Step 4

Add one side of the clasp to the loop by stringing it onto the short end of the wire until it nestles inside the loop.

Step 5

Wrap the wire tail around the long piece of wire. See pages 32–35 for additional details on wire wrapping techniques.

Step 6

Trim the excess wire from the wrap using the flush side of your wire cutters.

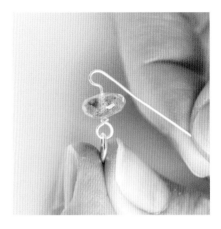

Step 7

String a bead onto the wire.

Step 8

Pinch the wire at the top of your bead with the round-nose pliers and bend the tail, creating a 90-degree angle.

Note: It is important to pinch the wire at the top of the bead BEFORE bending the wire. This will create the small space between your bead and the 90-degree angle needed to complete the loop.

Step 9

Repeat step 2 to make a question mark shape in the wire.

Step 13

Once you have reached your desired length, attach the remaining jump ring for the clasp to the last loop before completing the wraps.

Note: To add to the security of your bracelet, gently squeeze the ends of the clasp toward the center until all gaps are removed from the tips. This will keep the jump rings securely on your clasp.

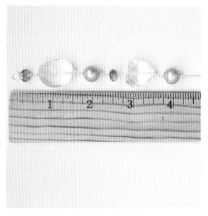

Step 10

Repeat step 3 to create the loop.

Step 11

Repeat steps 5–6 to finish the loop. You now have completed the first link in your bracelet. Repeat steps 1–3, attach your loop to your previous link, then repeat steps 5–11 to make each link in the bracelet.

Step 12

Keep track of your progress. The standard length for a bracelet is 7 inches (18 cm). Depending on the size of your wrist, you might want the final length to be slightly smaller or larger. If you have a centerpiece for your bracelet, use a ruler to mark your progress so that the centerpiece is placed appropriately.

Congratulations on completing your linked bracklet. This is a very versatile technique that can be used in a variety of jewelry designs. Earrings, bracelets, necklaces, and much more can be created using this simple construction method. Get creative with your own designs and have fun with it!

cable chain

Wire frame

Hammered finish

Natural Druzy

Stone Pendant

Tools

Flush wire cutters
Round-nose pliers
Flat-nose pliers
Steel block
Goldsmith hammer

Materials

7 inches (18 cm) wire, 16-gauge
1 teardrop stone with side-drilled
    hole at top, 20 × 30 mm
7 inches (18 cm) wire, 22-gauge
5 unsoldered jump rings, 4 mm
20 inches (51 cm) rolo chain,
    4 mm
1 lobster claw clasp, 5 mm
1 soldered jump ring, 5 mm

Helpful
Items

Ruler
Polishing cloth

Creating a wire frame for a necklace centerpiece can showcase greater skill as well as a more refined design. In the following project, you will create a secure and beautiful frame for a natural stone pendant.

SETTING UP

Prior to beginning your project, have all tools and materials ready. It is helpful to have a clean work space, clear of clutter and with proper lighting. This will make the process smoother and faster, and your materials won't get lost or misplaced. Make sure your steel block and hammer faces are in good condition, without marks or dents.

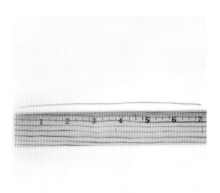

Step 1

Cut 7 inches (18 cm) of 16-gauge wire using the flush side of the wire cutters.

Step 2

Measure ⅝ inch (16 mm) from the end of the wire and pinch with the tips of the round-nose pliers. Make a 90-degree bend in the wire.

Step 3

Create a complete circle with the ⅝-inch (16 mm) end of wire by pinching the end of the wire with the round-nose pliers and rolling your wrist in the direction of your 90-degree angle.

  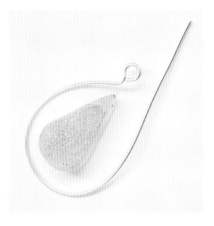

Step 4

Move the round-nose pliers beneath the loop and create a 45-degree angle with the long end of the wire.

Step 5

Continue to hold the round-nose pliers at the base of the loop, and use your fingers, along with the tension in the wire itself, to begin creating a teardrop shape.

Step 6

As you create the frame for your centerpiece, periodically check your progress against the shape of your stone. You want to ensure that the shape you are creating fits the size and shape of the stone. You also want to ensure you have ample room to hang the stone inside the wire frame.

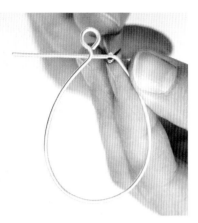

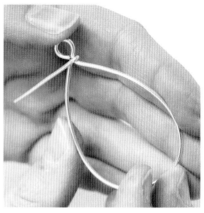

Step 7

Once you have achieved the desired shape, use flat-nose pliers to make a 45-degree bend in the wire where you want to close the frame. Bend the wire toward the loop.

Step 8

Using round-nose pliers, create a half circle in the wire tail, just past the bend. You are working toward creating a hook-type attachment that will close your frame.

Step 9

After creating a half circle, hook it around the other side of the frame, just beneath the original loop, as shown.

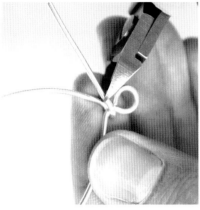 

Step 10

Trim the wire tail, leaving approximately ⅛ inch (3 mm) remaining.

Step 11

Using flat-nose pliers, begin turning the wire tail around the other side of your frame, using a circular motion with your wrist.

Step 12

Now that you have successfully shaped your frame, set up the steel block and goldsmith hammer. Make sure you have a clean work surface and the block and hammer are free of dust and debris.

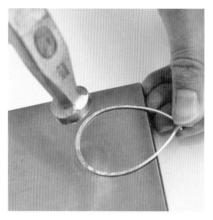

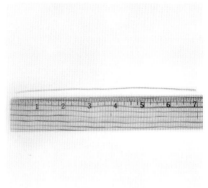

Step 13

Holding the top of the frame in your nondominant hand, begin hammering the bottom with the goldsmith hammer. This should be a swift and deliberate motion, bobbing the hammer up and down, similar to a piston.

Step 14

Begin hammering up both sides of your frame from the bottom center. The more you hammer your frame, the flatter and more spread out it will become. If you want the bottom center of your frame to appear more spread than the sides, then hammer that area more. Once the hammering is complete, polish the frame with a polishing cloth.

Step 15

Set your frame aside and cut a 7-inch (18 cm) length of 22-gauge wire.

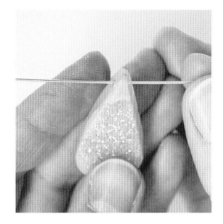  

Step 16

Center the stone bead on the wire.

Step 17

Fold both ends of the wire upward and pinch the wire at the top of the stone bead, creating two equal lengths.

Step 18

Make a 90-degree bend in both pieces of wire. You can do this with round-nose pliers or by simply placing your thumbnail above your stone bead and bending the wire over it.

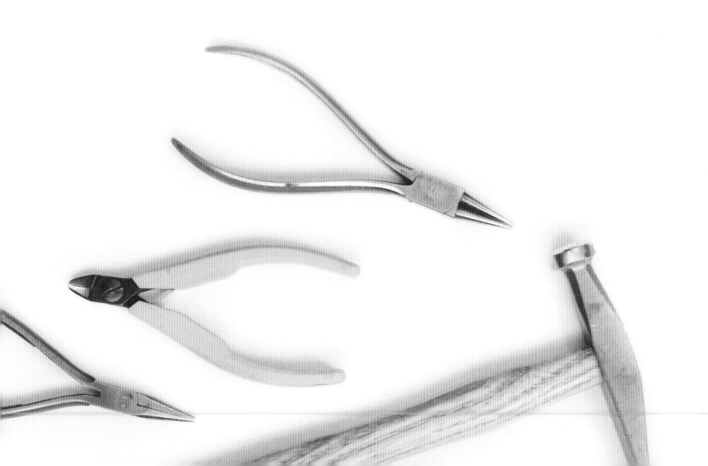

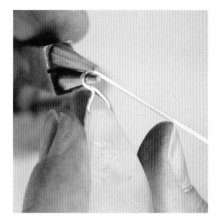

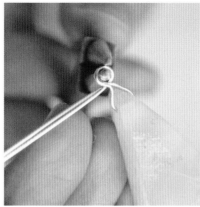

Step 19

Using round-nose pliers, create a question mark shape with both pieces of wire. See page 34 for additional details on how to execute this technique.

Step 20

Leaving one end of the round-nose pliers inside the question mark, create a full circle in the wires by pulling the wire tails toward the top of the bead stone.

Step 21

Begin wrapping the wire tails around the base of the loop. You can wrap the wire as many times as needed to fill the space between the loop and the stone.

Step 25

Use jump rings to attach a clasp and a soldered jump ring to opposite ends. Close the jump rings completely.

Step 26

Open a jump ring and attach the loop of the pendant frame. Don't close the jump ring.

Step 27

Center the pendant on the chain and close the jump ring. Add a second jump ring and close.

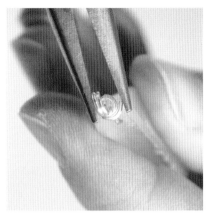

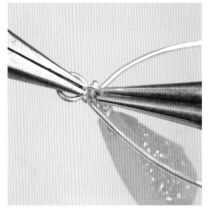

Step 22

Trim the wire tails using the flush side of the wire cutters.

Step 23

Secure the ends of the wire by using flat-nose pliers to gently squeeze the wires into the wrapped section. Be careful not to squeeze too hard, as this could deform your wire wrapping.

Step 24

Mount the stone inside the frame with a jump ring. Gently open the jump ring, attach the loops of the stone and frame to the jump ring, and close the jump ring (see page 45 for more information).

Your necklace is now complete! Creating wire frames for stones and beads is a fun way to design statement pieces on a budget. Practicing this technique will help you refine these skills over time. Consider using alternative metals to learn how those materials affect the construction process and overall design of your jewelry.

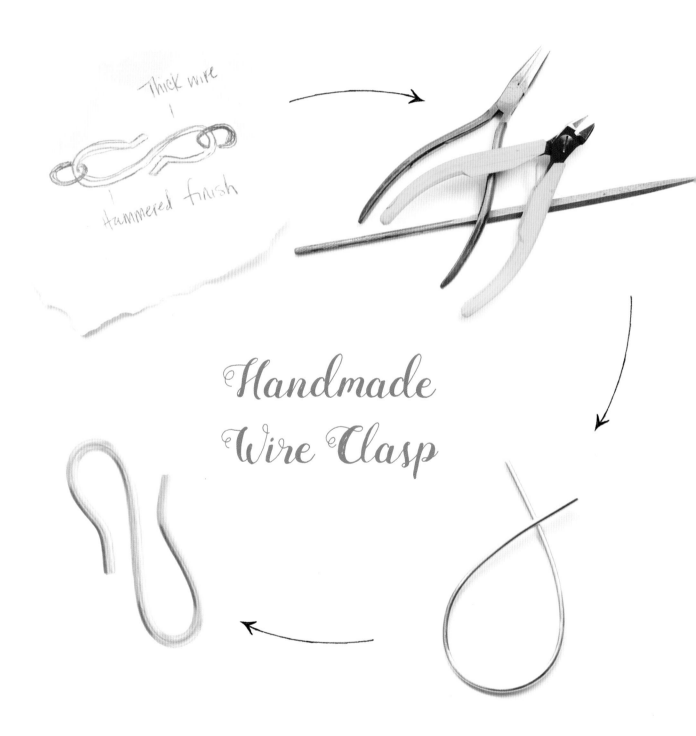

Thick wire

Hammered finish

Handmade Wire Clasp

Flush wire cutters

Flat needle-nose file

Flat-nose pliers

3 inches (7.6 cm) wire, 16-gauge

2 soldered jump rings, 6 mm

Ruler

Polishing cloth

In this project, you will discover one of the simplest ways to create your own handmade clasps. After becoming comfortable with this technique, you can explore additional shapes and designs for handmade clasps, a fun and inexpensive method to add originality to your jewelry.

SETTING UP

Prior to beginning your project, have all tools and materials ready. It is helpful to have a clean work space, clear of clutter and with proper lighting. This will make the process smoother and faster, and your materials won't get lost or misplaced.

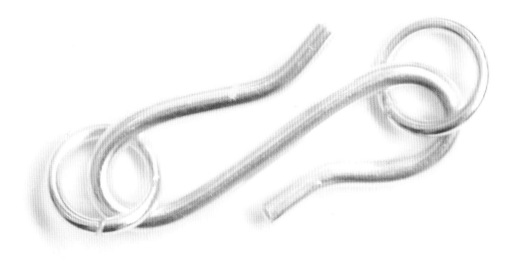

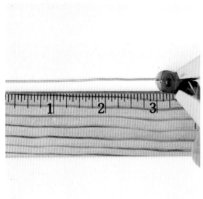  

Step 1

Using the flush wire cutters, cut a 3-inch (7.6 cm) piece of wire.

Step 2

Using a flat needle-nose file, file one end of the wire flat. Brace your arms against a table or jeweler's bench as you do this to effectively file metal.

Step 3

Tilting the wire slightly, remove any remaining rough edges from the ends.

Step 4

Using flat-nose pliers, pinch the end of the wire and create a 45-degree angle ¼ inch (6 mm) from the end.

Step 5

Holding the end of the wire with flat-nose pliers (adjusting your original grip from step 4 if needed), use your thumb to gently curve the wire.

Tip: I encourage you to practice using your fingers when forming the wire for this clasp. If you choose to use pliers to create all of the curves, you will end up with many dents and marks in the wire. If you do not have the ability, or machinery, to buff and polish the clasp once completed, use your fingers instead of pliers.

Step 6

Continuing to grip the wire with flat-nose pliers, create the center of the S-curve by using your forefinger. This may take some practice, so have patience as you learn this new technique.

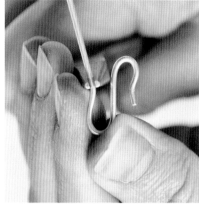

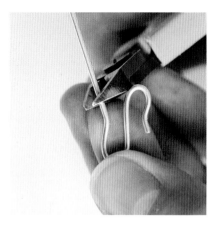

Step 7

Place your forefinger where the bottom curve of the clasp will be. Using your thumb, press the wire around the top of your forefinger, creating a gentle curve.

Step 8

Place the flat-nose pliers where you want the tail piece of the clasp to be. Just as you did in step 4, gently make a 45-degree bend in the wire.

Step 9

Using the flush side of the wire cutters, remove the excess wire from the clasp, creating two symmetrical ends.

Tip: The reason we cut the excess wire from the end of the clasp, instead of starting with a shorter piece, is because a longer piece of wire is much easier to hold and manipulate when creating free-form designs.

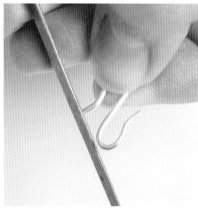
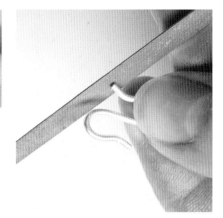
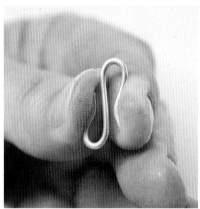

Step 10

Repeat step 2 on the second end of the clasp, creating a flat, or "flush," edge. Be careful not to touch the clasp with the file as you work. This may create scratches in the clasp that cannot be easily removed.

Step 11

Repeat step 3 and remove any sharp edges from the clasp, again taking care not to scratch the clasp with the file as you work. Once the shape of your clasp is complete, polish with a polishing cloth.

Step 12

Using your thumb and forefinger, gently squeeze the clasp together, creating a narrower, more aesthetically pleasing shape. Attach jump rings to both sides of the clasp by simply sliding the jump rings over the tip of the clasp, on each end, until the jump rings rest within the curves of the clasp. If possible, use soldered jump rings (jump rings without an opening) for additional strength and security.

Congratulations on completing your handmade wire clasp! There are many fun and interesting shapes you can use when making clasps from wire. When designing your own clasp, be conscious of how it will open and close, and consider how secure it will be. This is an easy and cost-effective way to create clasps for your jewelry while offering a unique signature to your designs.

Pearl Bracelet

Tools

Flush wire cutters
Flat-nose pliers
Round-nose pliers

Materials

Silk cord with needle attached,
   size 4
2 bead tips, 3 mm
1 lobster clasp, 5 mm
17 coin pearls, 10 mm
1 soldered jump ring, 4 mm

Helpful Items

Beading mat or small towel
Ruler
Jeweler's glue

I always recommend using silk when working with pearls. It is important that you purchase silk thread with the needle attached to the end of the thread. The silk product shown comes in a variety of colors and thread sizes. Pay attention to hole size in your pearls and be sure to purchase the correct thread size. I find thread size no. 4 to work best with most pearls.

SETTING UP

Prior to beginning your project, have all tools and materials ready. It is helpful to have a clean work space, clear of clutter and with proper lighting. This will make the process smoother and faster, and your materials won't get lost or misplaced. When working with white thread, it is important to have clean hands. This will prevent the thread from discoloring as you work with it.

Tip: When beginning any knotting project, it is important to practice first. See pages 36–41 in the Beginner Jewelry Techniques section for detailed instructions on knotting. Also, when working with any pearls or other round beads, it is helpful to work over a beading mat or a small hand towel to prevent your beads from rolling around as you work.

Step 1

Remove all of the thread from the card. Begin at one end of your thread and stretch your silk in small sections, working toward the other end of your thread. This is a very important step. If you don't pre-stretch your silk before stringing your bracelet, the weight of the beads will cause your silk to stretch over time, creating gaps in your jewelry.

Step 2

Tie a single overhand knot in the end of the thread opposite the needle. Pull the knot tight.

Step 3

Create a double overhand knot by tying a second knot directly over the first knot. Pull the knot tight.

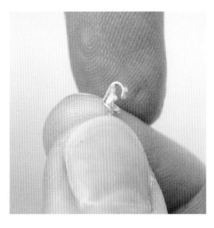

Step 4

With wire cutters, remove the thread tail after the knot. Do not trim too close to the knot or it will have a greater chance of becoming untied.

Step 5

String one of the bead tips onto the thread by placing the needle through the hole on the inside of bead tip base. If you have done this properly, the hook on the bead tip should face away from the long piece of thread, and the knot you created should nestle inside the bead tip base, as shown.

Step 6

Attach the hook on the bead tip to the lobster clasp. Using a pair of flat-nose pliers, gently squeeze the top of the hook and the bottom side of the cup to close the hook toward the base. Be sure to squeeze until the end of the hook reaches the base, completely closing any gaps.

Tip: The hooks on bead tips can be brittle. Squeeze gently, to avoid breaking them.

Step 7

String the first pearl, and slide it toward the clasp. Do not the force the beads onto the thread if the holes are too small. This will cause the needle to break away from the thread.

Step 8

Make a loose overhand knot close to the pearl. It is important that you begin with the knot as close to the pearl as possible. This will make it easier to tighten the knot against the pearl. See pages 38–39 in the Beginner Jewelry Techniques section for additional details.

Step 9

Position the knot between the pearl and your thumb and forefinger. Using your thumb and forefinger as tweezers, gently pull all remaining slack from the knot. Then use your thumbnail to tighten the knot further. This will ensure there is no slack remaining and will prevent your bracelet from developing space between the pearls over time.

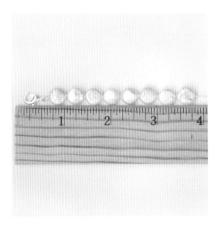  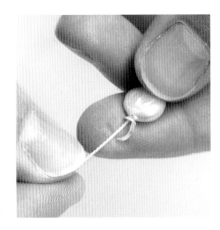

Step 10

Mark your progress with a ruler as you work. This is particularly helpful when attempting to create a symmetrical pattern. Standard bracelet lengths are 7 inches (18 cm). Adjust your bracelet length accordingly for smaller or larger wrists.

Step 11

Once you reached the desired length of your bracelet, prepare the second bead tip. Using round-nose pliers, gently open the hook. This will give you the space needed to tie a double knot inside the bead tip base.

Step 12

String the bead tip onto the thread by placing the needle through the hole in the bottom of the bead tip base. If you have done this correctly, the hook on the bead tip should be facing away from the pearls, as shown.

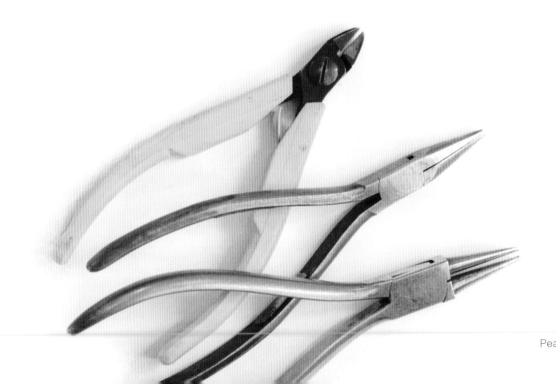

 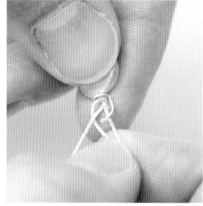 

Step 13

Tie a single overhand knot with the thread tail. Tighten the knot inside the base of the bead tip.

Step 14

Create a double overhand knot by tying a second knot directly over the first. It is important to loop the thread around the base of the first knot before the second knot is pulled tight. This will help you position the knots farther inside the bead tip base, once the thread is tightened.

Step 15

Remove the remaining thread by placing the flush side of the wire cutters against the knot. Do not trim the thread too close to the knot, as this could cause the knot to become untied.

 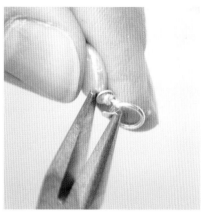

Step 16

Using round-nose pliers, gently re-form the hook in the bead tip. Be sure to leave the hook open.

Step 17

Attach the soldered jump ring to the bead tip hook. Again, using a pair of flat-nose pliers, gently squeeze the top of the hook and the bottom side of the cup to close the hook, being careful not to squeeze too tightly or vigorously.

Tip: It is helpful at this stage to apply a small amount of jeweler's glue to the inside of the bead tip. Do not apply too much glue, or you'll create a mess.

Congratulations on tackling the art of knotting and completing your bracelet! Do not expect to be perfect at this technique the first several times you attempt it. Knotting improves greatly with practice and is a method that provides a softness and fluidity that is unmatched by other construction methods. Knotting is always recommended when using pearls, to prevent them from becoming chipped over time and to avoid losing pearls if the thread breaks. Consider using knotting techniques with other types of beads to create a high-quality appearance with your jewelry designs.

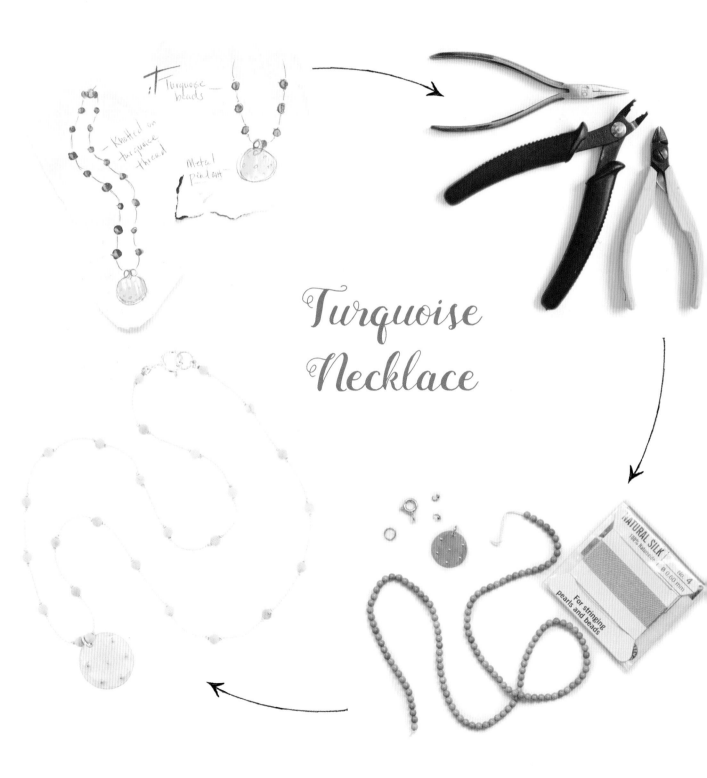

Turquoise beads

Knotted on turquoise thread

Metal pendant

Turquoise Necklace

NATURAL SILK
100% Naturseide   no. 4
ø 0.60 mm

For stringing pearls and beads

Flush wire cutters
Flat-nose pliers
Round-nose pliers

Silk cord with needle attached,
   size 4
2 bead tips, 3 mm
1 spring ring clasp, 5 mm
26 turquoise stone beads, 4 mm
1 soldered jump ring, 4 mm
Pendant (see the project on pages
   146–151 to create this pendant)

Beading mat or small towel
Ruler
Jeweler's glue

In this project you will review the execution of knotted jewelry, this time allowing space between your beads, which creates a feminine and delicate design. You can use any pendant of your choice, but the instructions to create the exact pendant shown can be found on pages 146–151. You need to make the pendant before stringing the beads.

SETTING UP

Prior to beginning your project, have all tools and materials ready. It is helpful to have a clean work space, clear of clutter and with proper lighting. This will make the process smoother and faster, and your materials won't get lost or misplaced. When working with thread it is also important to have clean hands. This will prevent the thread from discoloring as you work with it.

Note: It is important that you purchase silk thread with the needle already attached to the end of your thread. I prefer to use silk, but you can also use a nylon. Both silk and nylon come in a variety of colors and thread sizes. Pay attention to the size of the holes in your beads and be sure to purchase the correct thread size. I find thread size no. 4 to work best with most beads with standard size holes.

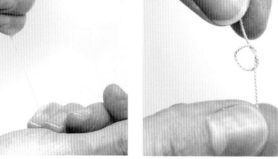
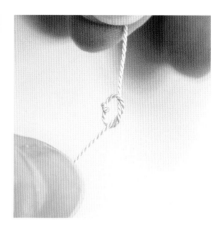

Step 1

Remove the entire thread from the card. Begin at one end of the thread and stretch the silk in small sections, working toward the opposite end. This is a very important step. If you don't pre-stretch the silk before stringing your necklace, the weight of the beads will cause the silk to stretch over time, creating gaps in your jewelry. If you are using nylon, it is not necessary to stretch the thread, and you can begin at step 2.

Step 2

Tie a single overhand knot in the end of the thread opposite the needle. Pull the knot tight.

Step 3

Create a double overhand knot by tying a second knot directly over your first. Pull the knot tight.

Step 4

With wire cutters, remove the thread tail. Do not trim too close to the knot or it will have a greater chance of becoming untied.

Step 5

String a bead tip onto the thread by placing the needle through the hole in the bead tip base. If you have done this properly, the hook on the bead tip should face away from the long piece of thread, and the knot you created should nestle inside the bead tip base, as shown.

Step 6

Attach the clasp to the hook of the bead tip.

  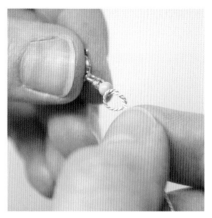

Step 7

Using a pair of flat-nose pliers, gently squeeze the top of the hook and the bottom side of the cup of the bead tip to close the hook toward the base. Be sure to squeeze until the end of the hook reaches the base, completely closing the hook.

Tip: The hooks on bead tips can be brittle. Squeeze gently to avoid breaking the hook.

Step 8

String the first bead, and slide it toward the clasp. Be sure not to force beads onto the thread if the holes are too small. This will cause the needle to break away from the thread.

Step 9

Make a loose overhand knot as close to the bead as possible. This will make it easier to tighten the knot against the bead.

 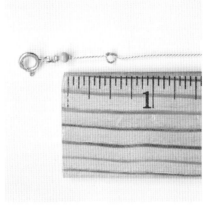 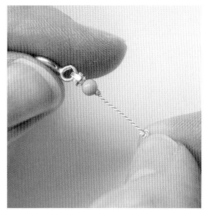

Step 10

Position the knot between the bead and your thumb and forefinger. Use your thumb and forefinger as tweezers and gently pull all the remaining slack from the knot. See pages 38–39 for further instructions.

Step 11

Create the next overhand knot and, using a ruler, position the knot approximately ½ inch (13 mm) from your previous one.

Step 12

Position the knot between the bead and your thumb and forefinger. Again, using your thumb and forefinger as tweezers, gently pull all the remaining slack from the knot, taking care to keep it in position along the length of the thread.

13

14

15

Step 13

String another bead. Slide the bead to the knot.

Step 14

Make a loose overhand knot as close to the bead as possible. This will make it easier to tighten the knot against the bead.

Step 15

Position the knot between the bead and your thumb and forefinger. Use the previously described methods to tighten the knot against the bead.

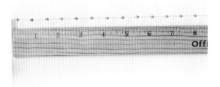

Step 16

Repeat steps 11–15 until you have reached the center of your necklace. For this project, we are creating a 16-inch (40.6 cm) necklace; therefore, 8 inches (20 cm) will mark the center. See page 169 for a necklace length chart.

Step 17

Attach the jump ring to the pendant (see pages 42–45 for directions). String the pendant and a bead onto the thread, as shown. It is important that the jump ring on the pendant be small enough to stay centered between the beads.

Step 18

Make a loose overhand knot close to the bead.

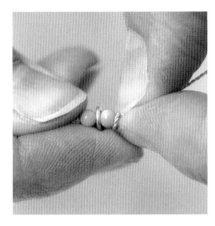

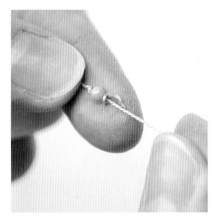

Step 19

Position the knot between the bead and your thumb and forefinger. Again, use previously described methods to tighten the knot against the bead. Continue with your series of knots and beads until you have reached the same length as the other side.

Step 20

Once you have reached the desired necklace length, prepare the remaining bead tip. Using round-nose pliers, gently open the loop on the end. This will give you the space needed to nestle the knots inside the bead tip base.

Step 21

String the thread needle through the hole in the bottom of the bead tip. If you have done this correctly, the hook on the bead tip should be facing away from the last bead, as shown.

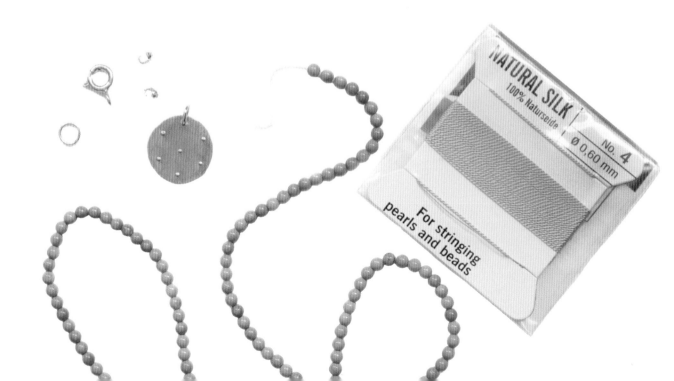

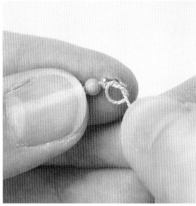 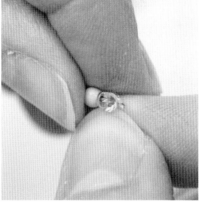 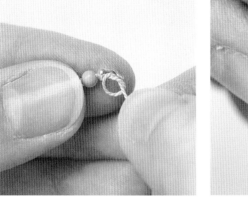

Step 22

Tie a single overhand knot with the thread tail and place it as close to the bead tip base as possible.

Step 23

Use your thumb and forefinger to gently tighten the knot inside the bead tip base.

Step 24

Create a double overhand knot by tying a second knot directly over the first knot. It is important to loop the thread around the base of the first knot before it is pulled tight. This will pull the knots further inside the bead tip base, once tightened.

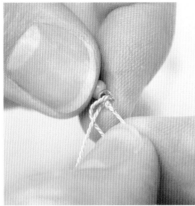 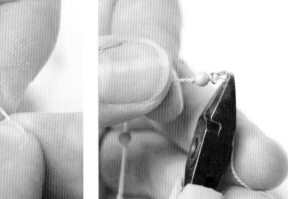 

Step 25

Use your thumb and forefinger to gently tighten the knot inside the bead tip base and remove any remaining slack in the knots.

Step 26

Cut the thread tail by placing the flush side of the wire cutters against the knot. Do not trim the thread too close to the knot, or it could cause the knot to come untied.

Step 27

Using round-nose pliers, gently re-form the hook in the bead tip. Don't close the bead tip at this time.

Step 28

Position the soldered jump ring
in the open bead tip hook. Again,
using flat-nose pliers, gently
squeeze the top of the hook and the
bottom side of the cup to close the
hook, being careful not to squeeze
too tightly or vigorously.

Tip: It is helpful at this stage to apply
a small amount of jeweler's glue to the
inside of the bead tip bases. Do not apply
too much glue to avoid permanently fixing
the clasp in place. The glue provides
added security so the knots do not
become untied.

Your necklace is now complete! You have successfully learned a technique
that is used in many modern jewelry designs and is extremely versatile.
This method can be used to create beautiful pieces of jewelry that reflect
refinement and sophistication.

*20 gauge wire

— Hammered finish

Hoop Earrings

Flush wire cutters
Round-nose pliers
Flat-nose pliers
Flat needle-nose file
Steel block
Goldsmith hammer

14 inches (35.6 cm) wire, 22-gauge

Ruler
Polishing cloth

The instructions for this project call for creating one earring at a time. If you prefer to make both earrings simultaneously, you will want to begin with two pieces of 22-gauge wire 7 inches (18 cm) long. Apply all instructions to both pieces prior to proceeding to the next step. Making both earrings simultaneously can help to ensure that they are well matched and close to identical. I recommend using hypoallergenic materials, such as silver or gold, when making earrings.

SETTING UP

Prior to beginning your project, have all tools and materials ready. It is helpful to have a clean work space, clear of clutter and with proper lighting. This will make the process smoother and faster, and your materials won't get lost or misplaced. When working with hammers, it is very important that the hammer surfaces are clean and free of dents and debris. Any dents in the hammer face or steel block will be imprinted onto your jewelry piece.

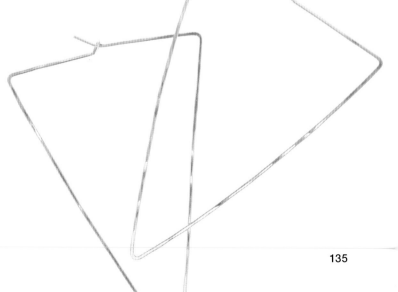

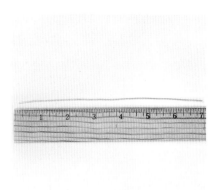

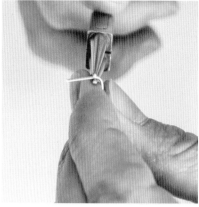

Step 1

Cut 7 inches (18 cm) of 22-gauge wire using flush wire cutters.

Step 2

Measure ⅜ inch (10 mm) from the end of the wire and make a 90-degree bend using round-nose pliers.

Step 3

Create a loop by pinching the end of the wire with round-nose pliers and rolling your wrist back toward the bend.

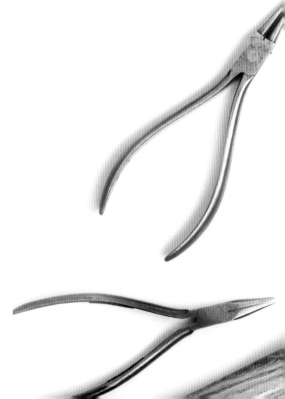

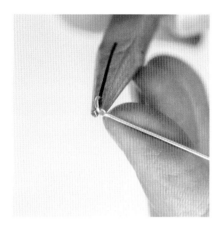

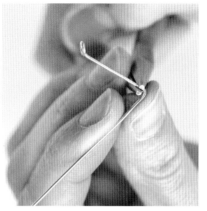

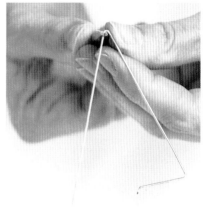

Step 4

Holding the circle, use flat-nose pliers to create a 45-degree bend at the base of the loop. If you have done this correctly, the long piece of wire will move toward the center of the circle, not to the side of the circle.

Step 5

Measure ¾ inch (2 cm) from the base of the loop and make a sharp 65-degree bend in the wire using flat-nose pliers. To properly execute this, pinch the wire with the flat-nose pliers at the ¾-inch (2 cm) mark and use your fingers to bend the wire directly next to the pliers.

Tip: In order to create a sharp bend, squeeze the wire with flat-nose pliers on both sides of the bend. This will eliminate any rounding of the wire that has taken place in the bending process.

Step 6

Measure 2½ inches (6.4 cm) from the previous bend. With the flat-nose pliers, make a sharp 50-degree bend in the wire using the techniques described in the previous step.

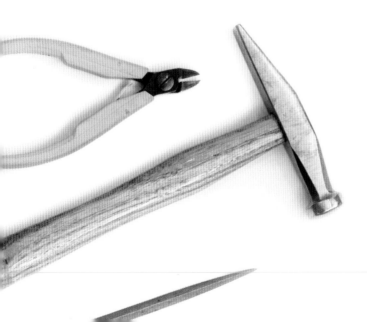

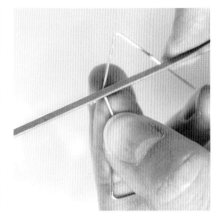

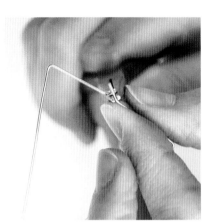

Step 7

Measure 2½ inches (6.4 cm) from your previous bend and make a sharp 100-degree bend in the wire using flat-nose pliers. Again, use the techniques described in step 5.

Step 8

Measure ¾ inch (2 cm) from your previous bend and make a sharp 45-degree bend in the wire using flat-nose pliers. This creates the end of the earring that will hook through the original loop, completing the earring's shape.

Note: If you have more than ¼ inch of wire left at the end of the earring, remove it with the flush wire cutters so the end will fit through the loop easily.

Step 9

File the end of the earring using a flat needle-nose file. Remove any sharp edges to avoid discomfort when putting the earring through the ear. Brace your arms against a table or jeweler's bench to effectively file metal.

Tip: It is helpful to file the end flat first, and then begin filing around the sharp edges to create a nice soft, rounded end.

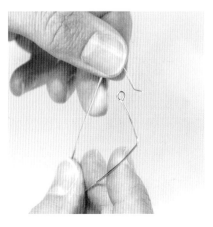

Step 13

Once hammering is complete, use your fingers to gently reshape the earring. Polish the earring with a polishing cloth to achieve a nice shine. Repeat steps 1–13 to create the second earring. Make sure each earring is symmetrical to the eye and that both earrings match.

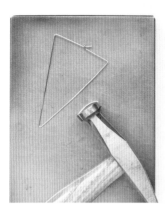

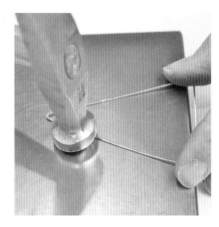

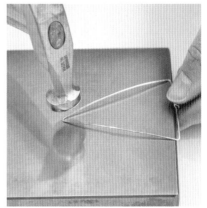

Step 10

Now that the shape of the earring is complete, set up the steel block and goldsmith hammer. Make sure you have a clean work surface and the block and hammer are free of dust and debris.

Step 11

Holding the top of the earring frame in your nondominant hand, begin hammering the earring with the goldsmith hammer. This should be a swift and deliberate up-and-down motion. Avoid hammering the top loop and tail piece.

Step 12

Finish hammering the entire surface of the first side. Then flip the earring over and hammer the other side. Continue to flip the earring back and forth and hammer each side until the frame is flat again. It is normal for the earring to bend as you hammer it. To counteract this, you simply hammer the opposite side.

Congratulations on completing your wire earrings! You can use this technique to create hoop earring of any shape and size. You can embellish wire hoop earrings with beads to give them a pop of color. Hoop earrings are timeless and are always on point with modern trends. This is an easy way to create high-fashion earrings with minimal tools and materials.

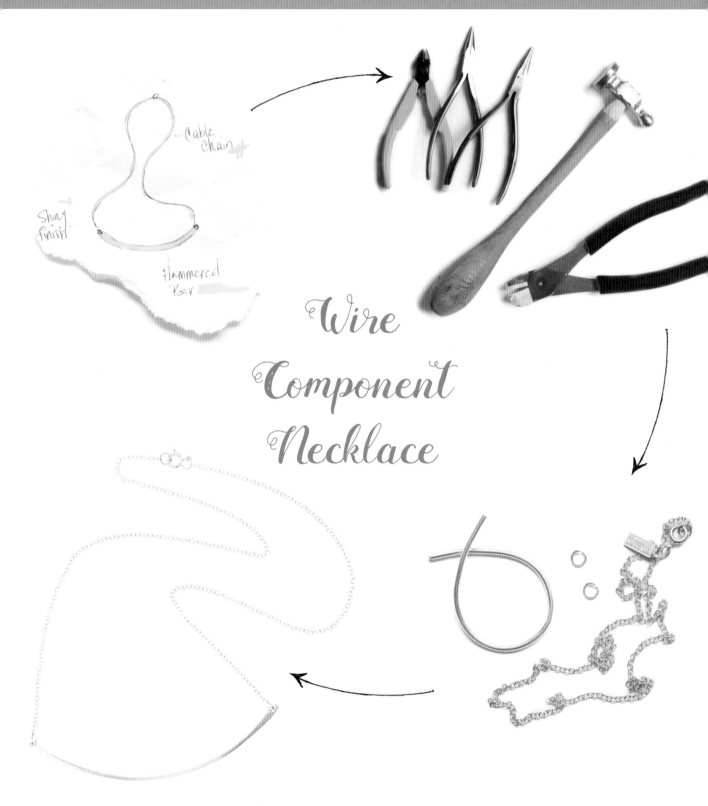

Cable Chain

Shiny Finish

Hammered Bar

Wire Component Necklace

Tools

Steel block
Goldsmith hammer
Flat needle-nose file
Hole-punching pliers
Flush wire cutters
2 pairs flat-nose pliers

Materials

3 inches (7.6 cm) wire, 14-gauge
16 inches (40.6 cm) cable chain
   necklace with clasp, 2 mm
2 jump rings, 4 mm

Helpful Items

Masking tape
Polishing cloth

Creating hammered components for jewelry is a fun and inexpensive way to make original and unique designs. This project shows the techniques for creating a simple yet sophisticated necklace.

SETTING UP

Prior to beginning this project, have a 3-inch (7.6 cm) piece of 14-gauge wire cut and ready. Have all tools and materials out and accessible. It is helpful to have a clean work space, clear of clutter and with proper lighting. This will make the process smoother and faster, and your materials won't get lost or misplaced. When working with hammers, it is very important that the hammer surfaces are clean and free of dents and debris. Any dents in your hammer face or steel block will be imprinted onto your jewelry piece.

 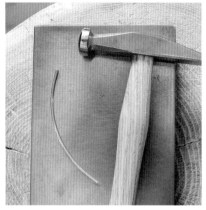 

Step 1

Using your hands, create a wide, soft curve in the 14-gauge wire. Avoid creating drastic bends in the wire by using gentle pressure as you work.

Step 2

Set up your steel block and goldsmith hammer. Have a clean work surface and check the block and hammer for dust and debris.

Step 3

Hold the wire against the steel block using your nondominant hand. Begin hammering the wire. This should be a swift and deliberate up-and-down motion. The curve in the wire will change slightly as you hammer. Take note of where you strike the wire with the hammer and how it affects the shape of the curve. You can begin hammering in either the center of the wire or at one end. Make sure your hammering is evenly distributed throughout the wire, and avoid hammering one section more than another.

Tip: For additional information on this technique and how hammers shape metal, research forging.

Step 4

Continue to move the wire as you hammer to create an evenly hammered surface.

Step 5

Once you have reached the desired finish, begin hammering each end of the wire until it is flared slightly. This will create enough surface area to punch holes in the ends for the jump rings. If you find the ends are not flaring, increase the force and frequency of your hammering.

Step 6

After you have successfully flared the ends of the wire, remove any sharp edges using a flat needle-nose file. It is important to brace your arms against a table or jeweler's bench as you file.

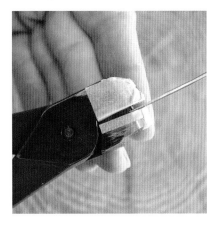

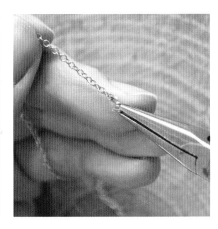

Step 7

Become familiar with the hole-punching pliers. Inside the tip is a small rod. Opposite the rod is a hole. The rod will produce the hole in the metal. It is helpful to wrap the tip of the pliers in masking tape. This will prevent the pliers from creating dents or markings in the metal as you punch holes. Put the small rod in the pliers directly in place for the desired hole. Squeeze the pliers until the rod pushes through the metal. Open the pliers and gently wiggle the metal free. Repeat this procedure to punch another hole in the opposite end of the wire.

Tip: You can also use a flex shaft or Dremel tool to drill a hole in metal. Because this book is for beginners, I focused on hole-punching pliers. Additionally, upon completion of step 7, you may choose to rub the wire with a polishing cloth to provide a nice shine to your necklace component.

Step 8

With wire cutters, cut the chain in half.

Step 9

Open a jump ring by twisting it with two pairs of flat-nose pliers (see pages 42–45). Attach one side of the wire component and one end of the open chain to the jump ring.

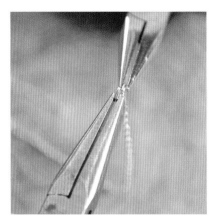  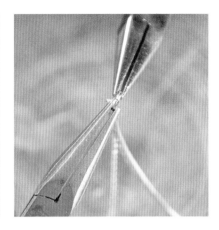

Step 10

Using flat-nose pliers, gently close the jump ring.

Step 11

Using a second jump ring, repeat step 9 on the other side of the wire with the second piece of chain.

Step 12

Again, using flat-nose pliers, gently close the jump ring.

Congratulations on completing your wire component necklace! This is a wonderful technique that can be used to create simple and sophisticated jewelry that reflects modern trends. Step outside of the box and apply this method to other jewelry items, such as earrings and bracelets.

raised bumps
+ satin finish

– Metal sheet
w/stamp details

*Rustic
Pendant*

Steel block
Goldsmith hammer
Steel dot stamp
Small piece of wood
Chasing hammer
Hole-punching pliers
Flat-nose pliers

1 sheet metal disk, 20-gauge,
⅝ inch (1.5 cm) diameter
1 jump ring, 5 mm

Black pen
Masking tape
Polishing cloth
Abrasive pad

Being able to create a handmade pendant will set your design abilities above those of a crafter. This hammered pendant is also used in the Turquoise Necklace on pages 122–133.

SETTING UP

Prior to beginning your project, have all tools and materials ready. It is helpful to have a clean work space, clear of clutter and with proper lighting. This will make the process smoother and faster, and your materials won't get lost or misplaced. When working with hammers, it is very important that the hammer surfaces are clean and free of dents and debris. Any dents in the hammer face or steel block will be imprinted onto your jewelry piece.

 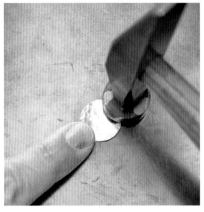 

Step 1

Set up the steel block and goldsmith hammer. Have a clean work surface and check to see that the block and hammer are free of dust and debris. Holding down the disk with your nondominant hand, begin hammering the disk with the goldsmith hammer. Use a swift and deliberate up-and-down motion.

Step 2

Move the disk as you hammer to create an even, hammered texture throughout. If you are not properly holding the disk as you hammer, it will move and jump around as you work.

Step 3

Using a fine-tipped black pen, mark the place where the hole for your jump ring will be punched. It is helpful to mark the front and back, as you will be working on both sides of the disk.

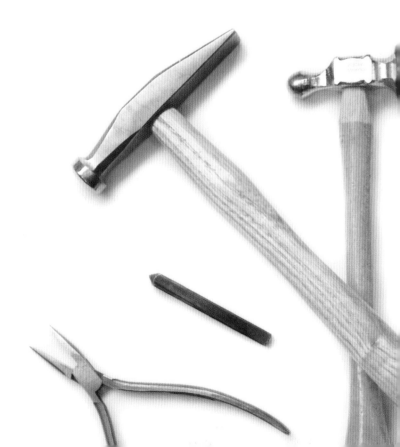

Step 4

Become familiar with the steel dot stamp. Identify the end with the small point, as this will be the end you place directly against the disk.

Step 5

Turn the disk so the back is facing upward, and place the hammered side facing down on a piece of wood. I use a large oak tree stump for this, but any small piece of wood will do for the size of this project. Place the steel dot stamp in the center of the disk. With the chasing hammer, make one swift and deliberate blow to the back of the stamp. This will create a small, circular dent in the center of the disk.

Note: I recommend using wood rather than a steel block, as this will create a more dramatic effect with the stamp on the opposite side of the metal. Research chasing and repoussé to gain a greater knowledge of this technique, though chasing and repoussé use a material called pitch instead of wood.

Step 6

Use the stamp to create markings around the outer edge of the back of the pendant, avoiding the mark where the hole will be punched.

Tip: Because the design is a bit rustic, it is not necessary to have perfect placements for the dots.

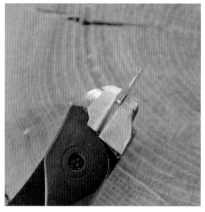

Step 7

Become familiar with the hole-punching pliers. Inside the tip of the pliers is a small rod. Opposite the rod is a hole. The rod will produce a hole in the metal. It is helpful to wrap the tip of the pliers in masking tape. This will prevent the pliers from creating dents or markings in the metal as you punch holes.

Note: If you are a bit more skilled in the art of jewelry making, you can also use a flex shaft or Dremel tool to drill a hole in the sheet. However, because this book is for beginners, I focused on hole-punching pliers.

Step 8

Align the disk so the small rod of the pliers is over the black dot of your disk. Squeeze the pliers until you feel the rod push through the metal. Open the pliers and gently wiggle the metal free.

Step 9

Decide what finish to give your pendant. For a shiny finish, gently rub the disk with a polishing cloth. I have created a satin finish by using a small piece of an abrasive pad. To create a satin finish, I recommend working in a back-and-forth motion so that the finish has a clean look. I find that applying a satin finish in a circular motion creates a messy appearance.

Tip: A satin finish is not easy to remove without proper buffing equipment. If you choose to add a satin finish, you must fully commit to this process and the outcome it creates.

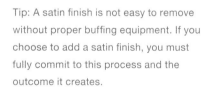

Step 10

Twist the jump ring open using flat-nose pliers. Avoid opening the jump ring by pulling it straight out. This will make it more difficult to close and will mar the shape and integrity of the jump ring once closed. You can read more details about how to open and close a jump ring on pages 42–45.

Step 11

Attach the jump ring to your pendant through the hole in the disk. Using flat-nose pliers, twist the jump ring closed.

Working with sheet metal and hammers is a fun and easy way to create jewelry of all kinds. This project provides only a very small tutorial on one of a wide variety of techniques. If you find you enjoy working with metal, I encourage you to research additional jewelry education programs. (See the Resources list on page 168 for continuing education courses.)

Stamped Letter Pendant

152

Tools

Steel block
Steel letter stamps: L, O, V, E
Chasing hammer
Hole-punching pliers
2 pairs flat-nose pliers

Materials

1 sheet metal disk, 20-gauge,
    ¾ inch (2 cm) diameter
1 jump ring, 4 mm
16 inches (40.6 cm) cable chain
    with clasp, 2 mm

Helpful Items

Polishing cloth
Masking tape
Abrasive pad

Letter stamping jewelry is an easy method to create personalized pieces that can be cherished for years to come. It's important to practice this technique often, because it is difficult for a novice to create even lettering.

SETTING UP

Prior to beginning your project, have all tools and materials ready. It is helpful to have a clean work space, clear of clutter and with proper lighting. This will make the process smoother and faster, and your materials won't get lost or misplaced. Check that the steel block is free of dents and debris. Any dents in the steel block surface will be imprinted onto your jewelry piece.

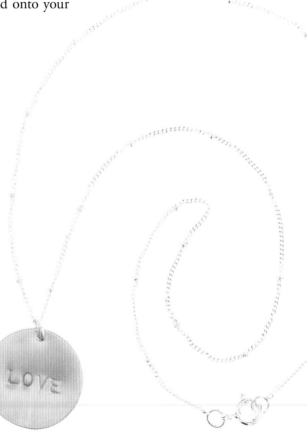

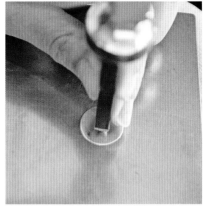

Step 1

Set up the steel block, steel letter stamps, and the chasing hammer. Have a clean work surface and check to see that the steel block is free of dust and debris. Select a sturdy surface that will allow minimal movement of the steel block while you apply the letters.

Step 2

Map out the placement of the letters on the pendant. Start in the center and work outward, toward the edge of the disk. For this project, you'll be stamping L-O-V-E. Place the letter "V" slightly to the right of the disk center. Hold the steel letter stamp in place and strike with the chasing hammer in one swift and deliberate motion.

Step 3

To keep the stamping even and symmetrical, place the letter "O" next, directly to the left of the "V." Use the same single, swift hammer motion, as in step 2.

 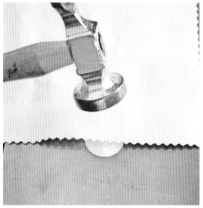 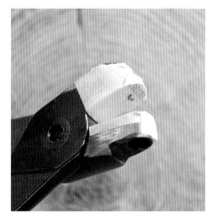

Step 4

Next, place the letter "E" to the right of the "V." Placing the last letter on the right of the pendant provides a better visual of the full design when you stamp the remaining letter to the left side of the pendant. Use the previously described methods to properly place and apply the "E."

Step 5

Next apply the letter "L." Complete the stampings, and then turn the disk face down on the steel block. Cover the disk with a piece of cloth and hammer lightly to remove any doming in the disk that occurred during the stamping process.

Step 6

Become familiar with the hole-punching pliers. Inside the tip of the pliers is a small rod. Opposite the rod is a hole. The rod will produce the hole in the metal. It is helpful to wrap the tip of the pliers in masking tape. This will prevent the pliers from creating dents or markings in the metal as you punch holes.

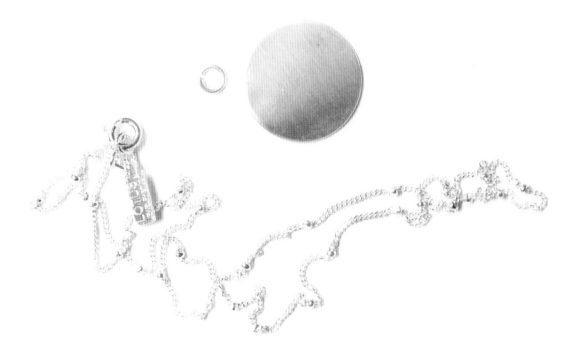

  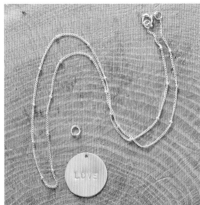

Step 7

Position the metal disk so that the small rod in the pliers is where you want the hole to be. Squeeze the pliers until you feel the rod push through the metal. Open the pliers and gently wiggle the metal free.

Step 8

Decide what finish to give your pendant. For a shiny finish, gently rub the disk with a polishing cloth. For this project, I have created a satin finish by using a small piece of abrasive pad. To create a satin finish, I recommend working in a back-and-forth motion so that the finish has a clean look. I find that applying a satin finish in a circular motion creates a messy appearance.

Tip: A satin finish is not easy to remove without proper buffing equipment. If you choose to add a satin finish, you must fully commit to this process and the outcome it creates.

Step 9

Prepare to assemble the necklace by placing the pendant, jump ring, and necklace onto your work surface.

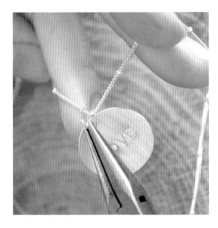 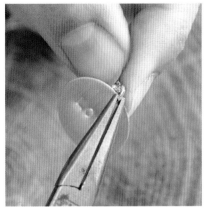

Step 10

Twist the jump ring open using flat-nose pliers. Avoid opening the jump ring by pulling it straight out. This will make it more difficult to close and the jump ring will lose its shape and integrity.

Step 11

String the jump ring through the hole in the pendant and around the chain. Using flat-nose pliers, twist the jump ring closed.

Congratulations on completing your stamped letter necklace! You may find this technique to have its own set of challenges. Having a sturdy surface, and hammering with vigor, will provide the best results. Try practicing with inexpensive material to become more proficient. Stamping provides a wonderful way to create personalized jewelry and gifts for any special occasion.

Flower stamps

Cable chain

oxidized finish

Stamped Designs

Steel block
Steel stamps of choice
Chasing hammer
Flat needle-nose file
Hole-punching pliers
Flush wire cutters
2 pairs flat-nose pliers

1 sheet metal rectangle, 20-gauge,
    ¼ × 1½ inches (6 mm × 3.8 cm)
2 jump rings, 4 mm
16 inches (40.6 cm) cable chain
    with clasp, 2 mm

Masking tape
Liquid sulfur
Toothpick or cotton swab
Polishing cloth

This project features techniques similar to those used in the previous project, Stamped Letter Pendant (pages 152–157). You will use design stamps to create unique and artistic jewelry elements. This is a very popular method used in Native American jewelry.

SETTING UP

Prior to beginning your project, have all tools and materials ready. It is helpful to have a clean work space, clear of clutter and with proper lighting. This will make the process smoother and faster, and your materials won't get lost or misplaced. Check that the steel block is free of dents and debris. Any dents in the steel block surface will be imprinted onto your jewelry piece.

Step 1

Set up the steel block, the steel stamps, and the chasing hammer. Have a clean work surface and check to see that the steel block is free of dust and debris. Select a sturdy surface that will allow minimal movement of the steel block while applying the stamps.

Step 2

Map out the placement of the design for your pendant. Start in the center and work outward. This will help keep the design symmetrical as you work. Hold the steel letter stamp in place and strike it with the chasing hammer in one swift and deliberate motion.

Step 3

Continue stamping until your design is complete. If your stamps aren't as clear as you'd like, try using an alternative surface under the steel block. If the stamps are bouncing on the metal when you strike the hammer, you either need to apply a stronger blow with the hammer or provide a sturdier surface for the steel block.

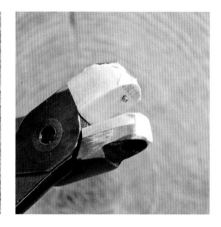

Step 4

File the corners of the pendant using a flat needle-nose file, removing any sharp edges. It is important to brace your forearms against a table or jeweler's bench in order to effectively file your pendant.

Step 5

Continue filing all four corners until they match, for the most part, in appearance. They don't need to be perfect.

Step 6

Become familiar with the hole-punching pliers. Inside the tip of the pliers is a small rod. Opposite the rod is a hole. The rod will produce the hole in the metal. It is helpful to wrap the tip of the pliers in masking tape. This will prevent the pliers from creating dents or markings in the metal as you punch holes.

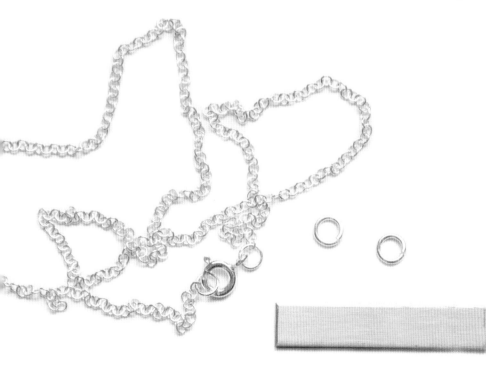

Step 7

Insert the metal pendant, aligning the small rod in the pliers where you want the hole to be. In this project the holes will be in the top corners on both ends of the pendant. Squeeze the pliers until you feel the rod push through the metal. Open the pliers and gently wiggle the metal pendant free. Punch a second hole on the other side of the pendant.

Step 8

Decide on the finish for your necklace. Sterling silver is easily blackened using a liquid sulfur solution, commonly found at any jewelry supply store. Use a toothpick or cotton swab to apply the solution to the metal. If you choose an alternative finish for your necklace, you can skip to step 12.

Step 9

The photo shows all the designs with the sulfur solution applied. After applying liquid sulfur to your design, rinse thoroughly with water and dry the pendant.

Step 13

Repeat step 12 on the opposite side of the necklace component, using the second jump ring.

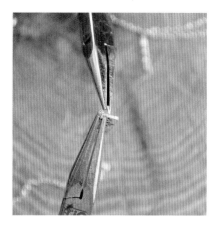

Step 10

Polish the pendant, using a polishing cloth, until only the black in the stamped design remains. Apply significant pressure with the cloth to remove any unwanted blackening. The longer the solution is left on the metal, the more difficult it will be to remove, so polish the pendant immediately after applying and rinsing the liquid sulfur solution.

Step 11

Continue polishing until you have reached your desired finish.

Step 12

Prepare to assemble the necklace by severing the chain with wire cutters, centering the cut between the chain's clasp and its opposite ring, creating an opening to mount the centerpiece. Open one jump ring by twisting it using two pairs of flat-nose pliers. Use a jump ring to attach one side of the pendant to the open chain. Twist the jump ring closed.

Congratulations on completing the final project in this book! We have covered a wide range of techniques, and I hope you have gained greater knowledge in the art of jewelry making. I encourage you to be creative in your future jewelry projects, and hope that you strive to create unique jewelry that reflects skill and quality while showcasing good design and a sense of refinement.

Turning Your Craft into a Business

Many people with hobbies have considered turning their craft into a business at one point or another. Some become too overwhelmed to take that first leap of faith; some make attempts, fail, and get discouraged; and others become wildly successful! I want to share some tips I've learned over the years that will, hopefully, set you up for success. Through hard work and dedication, I turned my basement business, Lotus Jewelry Studio, into a booming company that supplies products internationally—with a large team of jewelers and more than 70 sales reps behind me. You can, too!

Number 1: Master Your Craft

In business, excellent products stand out from the rest. Consumers have an eye for quality, so naturally your products will sell if they are constructed properly and demonstrate talent and refinement. You may also find that as your company grows, your products and creation process are questioned and challenged from time to time. It will benefit you to have an impressive level of knowledge in your field so that you can fully stand behind your company and the products it sells. There will always be many people who do what you do. One of the things that will set you apart from the rest is being REALLY good at your craft.

Number 2: Know Your Numbers

I cannot stress enough how important it is to successfully manage your company's finances. If finances are not your strength, I strongly encourage you to enroll in an accounting class. Local community colleges often offer inexpensive courses. You will thank yourself for taking this crucial step in structuring your business. Accounting is the backbone of any company. If you don't have the knowledge to properly manage money, your company won't have a solid structure to rest upon. After taking a class, if you still feel money management is not your strength, hire someone who is skilled in these matters. There are many accountants who help small businesses for a nominal monthly fee.

Number 3: Write a Business Plan

Writing a business plan enables you to easily define the structure of your company. This is an important step because you will be faced with many decisions before getting started. Who will be your customers. Do you sell wholesale or retail? Where will you source your materials? What is your start-up budget? What kind of facility do you need? Do not let these questions scare you. Maybe your starting facility is your basement or guest bedroom—that's okay! Many successful companies began as home businesses. You don't have a start-up budget? Neither did I, and I have made it very far in business by properly managing money, taking healthy risks, and knowing how to grow my company. Be creative with your business plan. It should be unique and reflect your dreams and vision. Have fun with it!

It is also crucial in the start-up phase to decide upon what type of entity your company will be. State governments have public information about partnerships, limited liability companies (LLCs), corporations, and so on. It is important to choose the correct structure for your company and its future goals. I found it to be beneficial in the beginning to seek the advice of a certified public accountant

(CPA). Many small businesses start as LLCs, but it is extremely important to know the tax structures for each entity prior to filing your business with the state and federal government.

Number 4: Register Your Business

You've spent nights in bed dreaming of the perfect business name only to find it is already taken. If you do not plan to operate your business in the near future, register your trade name anyway. It is very inexpensive and can be done through your local courthouse. The same goes for your website. Some web addresses can be difficult to secure, so choose a hosting site (for example, GoDaddy.com, HostGator.com, and LiquidWeb.com) and register your domain name. You can easily search online to find the necessary information for your state to legally register your small business (for example, in Maryland, the website is Maryland.gov). Once you have chosen a business entity, you will need a valid business license. This can also be done through your state. You can consult a small business lawyer's advice if you are daunted by the process of legally establishing your business. And last, I encourage you to set up a business bank account that will be separate from your personal account in order to properly manage your company's funds. Don't cut corners. Be thorough and create a foundation for success!

Number 5: Selling Your Product(s)

You've spent months making products . . . now what? If you are starting out small, look into local craft fairs or other venues that allow independent vendors. There are online websites that allow artists to sell their goods for a small fee, the most popular being Etsy.com. You can also solicit local shop owners to buy your products or allow you to sell on consignment. This is a great way to get started if you are looking to create a start-up budget from scratch.

If you are hoping to take a larger leap out of the gate, you might want to consider selling wholesale at an industry trade show. Industry trade shows are large-scale venues where companies, large and small, showcase their products to sell to store owners for a select amount of time. The benefit of selling to industry buyers is you acquire a larger number of orders and open yourself to repeat business. You also broaden your customer base, as the attendees at these shows travel from all over the world to attend to buy the latest and greatest products. These trade shows are usually quite expensive, so make sure you plan properly for success if investing in this avenue. A simple web search can steer you in the right direction when choosing a trade show that best suits your business.

Number 6: Ask for Help

They say "a jack of all trades is a master of none." Do not expect yourself to be great at everything. Focus on what your strengths are and ask for help with the rest. That help may be in the form of taking a small business class. Or maybe you have a family member who is an accessories buyer for a large retailer. Reach out to that person! In business you will find that people often ask for favors. If you are asking for favors, you MUST be open to reciprocating over time. What you give, you get. You never know when you will need that favor to be repaid.

Number 7: Have Fun!

It is important to remember to have fun when getting your business off the ground. I am not going to lie: it is going to be a LOT of hard work and countless hours dedicated to your mission. However, it is important to always remember why you decided to turn your craft into a business in the first place. You may want freedom with your time or money. You gain both of these and more once you get yourself established. I have seen many business owners close up shop over the years because they lost the fun. Always keep your eye on the prize and keep your thoughts positive! Be your own cheerleader and others will support you as well.

Lotus Jewelry Studio's first industry trade show.

Model photo shoot for 2016 collection.

Lotus Jewelry Studio's current trade show display.

Resources

Suppliers

Please support local businesses whenever possible. Here is a short list of amazing stores I have visited.

California

Beads, Crystals & More
Encinitas, CA
www.beadscrystalsandmore.com

Colorado

Nomad Bead Merchants
Boulder, CO
www.nomadbeads.com

Maryland

Beadazzled
Baltimore, MD
www.beadazzled.com

New Mexico

Beadweaver
Santa Fe, NM
www.beadweaverofsantafe.com

New York

Beads World
New York, NY
www.beadsworldusa.com

National Suppliers

Michaels Craft Stores
www.michaels.com

A.C. Moore
www.acmoore.com

Hobby Lobby
www.hobbylobby.com

Jo-Ann Fabric & Craft Stores
www.joann.com

Continuing Jewelry Education

For me, jewelry education began at an early age. It was rooted in the art of beading and brewed a curiosity in me that has carried me throughout my life. Many people's first experience in beading can spark a strong interest in furthering their knowledge about jewelry making. In college, I managed a bead store (Beads, Crystals & More in Encinitas, CA) and taught many beginner classes so that others could explore their passion for the craft. Many local bead stores offer a wide variety of classes on beading, and I encourage you to research these opportunities. After mastering a range of beading techniques, I had a strong desire to learn more about metalsmithing and becoming a jeweler. If you find yourself with the same passion, I highly encourage you to research the following schools:

Revere Academy of Jewelry Arts
San Francisco, CA
www.revereacademy.com

Gemological Institute of America (GIA)
Carlsbad, CA
www.gia.edu

Creative Side Jewelry Academy of Austin
Austin, TX
www.creativeside.org

Charts

Sheet Gauge Chart

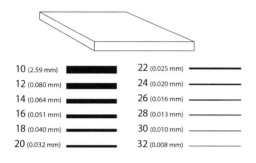

10 (2.59 mm) ▬▬▬▬	22 (0.025 mm) ▬▬▬▬
12 (0.080 mm) ▬▬▬▬	24 (0.020 mm) ▬▬▬▬
14 (0.064 mm) ▬▬▬▬	26 (0.016 mm) ▬▬▬▬
16 (0.051 mm) ▬▬▬▬	28 (0.013 mm) ▬▬▬▬
18 (0.040 mm) ▬▬▬▬	30 (0.010 mm) ▬▬▬▬
20 (0.032 mm) ▬▬▬▬	32 (0.008 mm) ▬▬▬▬

Wire Gauge Chart

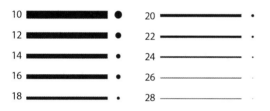

10 ●	20 •
12 ●	22 •
14 ●	24 •
16 ●	26 •
18 ●	28 •

Thread Size Chart

Spools	Cards	Ø in mm
	#0	0.30
6/F		0.35
	#1	0.35
8/FFF		0.42
	#2	0.45
	#3	0.50
2-ply 6/F		0.53
	#4	0.60
2-ply 8/FFF		0.63
	#5	0.65
	#6	0.70
3-ply 6/F		0.70
	#7	0.75
	#8	0.80
3-ply 8/FFF		0.84
	#10	0.90
	#12	0.98
	#14	1.02
	#16	1.05

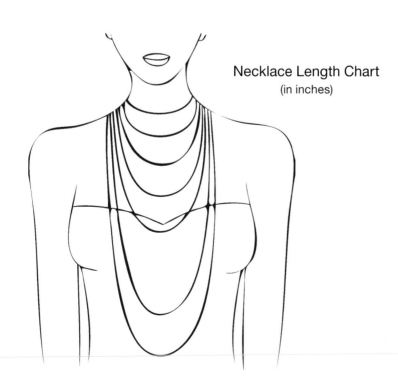

Necklace Length Chart
(in inches)

Briolette Stone Chart

A. Lapis

B. Garnet

C. Aqua chalcedony

D. Ruby chalcedony

E. Pyrite

F. Clear quartz

G. Smoky quartz

H. Purple mystic topaz

I. Prehnite

J. Blue chalcedony

K. Black spinel

L. White moonstone

M. Carnelian

N. Champagn quartz

O. Labradorite

P. Turquoise

Q. Rose quartz

R. Amethyst

S. Lemon quartz

T. Chrysoprase

A   B   C D

E   F   G   H

I   J   K   L

M   N   O   P

Q   R   S T

Bead Size Chart

Bead Diameter		Bead Length
2 mm	•	2 mm = 1/16″
3 mm	•	3 mm = 3/32″
4 mm	•	4 mm = 1/8″
5 mm	●	5 mm = 3/16″
6 mm	●	6 mm = Just under 1/4″
7 mm	●	7 mm = Just over 1/4″
8 mm	●	8 mm = 5/16″
9 mm	●	9 mm = Just under 3/8″
10 mm	●	10 mm = Just over 3/8″
11 mm	●	11 mm = 7/16″
12 mm	●	12 mm = Just under 1/2″
13 mm	●	13 mm = Just over 1/2″
14 mm	●	14 mm = 9/16″
15 mm	●	15 mm = Just under 5/8″
16 mm	●	16 mm = 5/8″

Bead Shape Chart

 Round

 Bicone

 Teadrop

 Oval

 (Curved) Tube

 Bugle

 E-Bead

 Seed Bead

About the Author

I was born in Encinitas, California, a small beach town located in San Diego County. Encinitas is best known for its laid-back atmosphere and endless sunshine, and is bustling with surfers, hippies, and yogis. I spent countless hours as an adolescent scouring the beaches for shells and other found objects that could be made into jewelry. As I grew older, jewelry became a strong passion, and you could often find me in the local bead shops. After high school I went on to study music, but my passion for jewelry was always present and I ultimately decided to leave school to pursue my dream of being a jeweler.

In 2001, I moved to San Francisco and enrolled at the Revere Academy of Jewelry Arts. It was during my studies there that I realized, wholeheartedly, that I had found my calling. I spent the better part of two years studying the art of jewelry making, which included soldering, stone setting, casting, forging, wax carving, jewelry repair, gemology, and much more. During my time in San Francisco I was able to refine my craft and skills in preparation for making a career as a jeweler.

Upon receiving my degree as a Graduate Jeweler from the Revere Academy, I moved to San Diego and worked in fine jewelry stores, executing repairs and custom work. In 2004, I met my husband, Erik, who is also a fine jeweler, and in 2006 we moved to his hometown of Baltimore, Maryland, where we still live today. Shortly after our wedding in 2006 we started our company, Lotus Jewelry Studio. We had no idea then that what started as a basement business would one day take us to the most amazing cities around the world and provide us with incredible experiences, meeting fascinating people and reaching success beyond our wildest dreams.

Today, Lotus Jewelry Studio is strong and thriving! Our jewelry is sold to thousands of retailers worldwide, and we continue to grow our brand every year. Our products are still made by hand in our Baltimore-based facility and we currently employ many amazing artists.

Gratitude is almost too small of a word to describe how I feel about my life. A childhood hobby that began almost three decades ago has brought me to this place in my life where I get to work in a creative environment and live out my passion in ways I had only dreamed of.

—Courtney Legenhausen

Index